COUNTDOWN

TO THE

SHOWDOWN

Dwight K. Nelson

Hart Research Center
Fallbrook, California

Edited by Ken McFarland
Cover design by Ria Fisher
Cover illustrations by Nathan Greene

ISBN 1-878046-09-8

Contents

Also Available From Hart Research Center iv

Foreword v

About the Author viii

Preface ix

Acknowledgments xiii

1. How to Stalk a Dragon 17

2. Beauty and the Beast 29

3. Is the New Christian Right Wrong? 49

4. A Loyalty That Could Get You Killed 67

5. Showdown of the Gods 87

6. When the Heat's on Hot 103

7. I Saw Jesus Coming 119

Afterword 127

ALSO AVAILABLE FROM HART RESEARCH CENTER

In addition to this book and the accompanying
cassette album, other outreach resources
are available from Hart Research Center.

For information, write:
Hart Research Center
P.O. Box 2377
Fallbrook, CA 92088

Or call:
(619) 723-8082 [pricing and other information]
(800) 487-4278 [orders *only*, please!]

Foreword

We are living in momentous and uncertain times. If ever there were a time when the cry of a desperate world summoned the church to fulfill its divinely ordained role as a watchman, surely this is that hour. How can an informed Christian today not hear—in the anxiety-ridden clamor of our age—an echo of the ancient query, "Watchman, what of the night? Watchman, what of the night?" (Isaiah 21:11)?

Surely the time has come for the church to take literally its divine commission to "blow the trumpet to warn the people . . . Son of man, I have made you a watchman for the house of Israel; so hear the word I speak and give them warning from me" (Ezekiel 33:3, 7). "Again," the New Testament evangelist reiterated, "if the trumpet does not sound a clear call, who will get ready for battle?" (1 Corinthians 14:8).

What you are about to read is the voice of a watchman on the walls trumpeting a warning cry. The author, Dwight K. Nelson, was a student of mine during his doctoral studies, and for the past nine years, he has been the senior pastor of the university church of which I am a member. When I first heard the chapters of this book preached as a series of sermons, I could sense an urgent, prophetic appeal both to the church and to the world, warning of the approaching apocalyptic showdown. And I was not alone. A full house for mid-week prayer meetings and full double services for worship every Sabbath day were indications that the message of the Apocalypse today strikes a responsive chord in modern, sophisticated minds.

As one who was reared a Roman Catholic and later joined the Seventh-day Adventist Church, I have long been keenly interested in Scripture. As a student of the Apocalypse and as one who teaches from it here at the Seminary, I note that today it is not only churchgoers who with increased interest are returning to the Book. I see in the faces of secular humanity a numinous hunger to know the meaning of the unprecedented and momentous events of our times. Which makes *Countdown to the Showdown* so timely. Those who turn to these pages will hardly ever be able to read the headlines of the daily news in the same way again.

As I first heard this series of sermons, and even more so as I read the manuscript, I sensed the potential that this book has to help unmask end-time characters, expose secret alliances, and identify alarming trends that are foreshadowed in the Apocalypse. It does so convincingly and compellingly. And yet, behind its hard-hitting style lies the compassionate pastoral heart of its author. Having known Dwight for many years, I am certain that *Countdown to the Showdown* was born out of his love for his church and the world around him.

And that sets this book apart. For there are some independent voices today that are recklessly making strident and critical allegations based on the Apocalypse. On the other hand, some have written with such a fear of offending anyone that they have muted the urgent summons from the divine throne room to a sleeping planet. *Countdown to the Showdown* avoids both extremes.

As a minister of the Seventh-day Adventist Church, the

author writes out of a spiritual heritage whose prophetic understanding, while rare in its modern application, is rooted deeply in the historical Protestant interpretation of the Apocalypse. Indeed, in *Countdown to the Showdown*, I sense the fires of conviction, once stoked by the Holy Spirit to give birth to the Reformation, still aflame today. That flame must spread if the church is to fulfill its divinely ordained mission of alerting the world to the soon return of Jesus Christ.

While the author shows how present events point to the soon fulfillment of the final events prophesied in the Apocalypse, he makes no attempt to set dates for such. Rather, his book is a carefully reasoned, cogent analysis of current events in the context of rapidly fulfilling prophecy. Not only is the subject itself captivating and gripping, but the creative writing style of *Countdown to the Showdown* carries the reader with pulse-quickening examination from one chapter to the next.

I believe the time has come for such a book. "The night is almost over, the day is almost here" (Romans 13:12). May the soon-coming Lord of the Apocalypse be the bright Hope of every reader.

Raoul Dederen, Ph.D.
Seventh-day Adventist Theological Seminary
Andrews University
Berrien Springs, Michigan

ABOUT THE AUTHOR

Dwight K. Nelson is the senior pastor of the Pioneer Memorial Church of Seventh-day Adventists on the campus of Andrews University in Berrien Springs, Michigan. He began his pastorate there in 1983, and also serves as adjunct professor for homiletics at the Andrews University Seventh-day Adventist Theological Seminary.

Prior to his coming to Pioneer Memorial, Dwight served as a pastor for ten years in the state of Oregon, where he was ordained to the gospel ministry in 1979. He received his bachelor of arts degree in 1973 from Southern College in Collegedale, Tennessee, his master of divinity degree from Andrews University in 1976, and his doctor of ministry degree in 1986—also from Andrews.

For two years, Dr. Nelson produced and narrated a radio program entitled "Perception." He is currently the speaker of a television series called "Perceptions."

Born in Toyko, Japan, of missionary parents, Dwight speaks fluent Japanese. He is married to Karen Oswald Nelson—a registered nurse. They have a son, Kirk—and a daughter, Kristin.

Preface

Thomas Carlyle, the great English philosopher, found himself one evening in a house full of guests, attending a New Year's Eve party in a home in northern England. As the evening dragged on, the idle chit-chat and frivolous banter of the party-goers began to wear on his soul. Deciding to leave the crowd to its dance and song, Carlyle slipped out of the house and stepped into a black and ominous night, the silver stars shut away by angry storm clouds that spanned the night sky. A chill and moaning wind tore at the cloak he had pulled tightly about himself.

Through the darkness, Carlyle found his way down to the pounding sea until, at last and alone, he stood on the English shore. As the windswept breakers crashed at his feet, the midnight thunders roared over his head, the blackness of the sky spilled into the darkness of the deep, and the old year vanished before the new, the soul of the great philosopher, caught up in the enormity of it all, cried out: **"I stand at the center of immensities, at the conflux of eternities!"**

Is it any different for us today—we who stand on the

ragged shoreline of events made so instantly out of date that our headlines—and even our maps—can no longer keep up? How else shall we portray the recent months that the howling winds of time have bequeathed us? Have we not come to that fated hour when we, like the ancient prophet and his people, must now "reap the whirlwind"? (Hosea 8:7.)

Carlyle, wearied by the idle party, cried out: "I stand at the center of immensities, at the conflux of eternities!" Because, you see, the party is over. It is time to leave the dance and song behind. Time to step out of the cozy, careless crowd. Time, high time, to step into the gathering midnight storm of a planet and a civilization on an irrevocable collision course with eternity.

Look back at the astounding days you and I survived during those headline-shattering months of the year 1991. The somber visages of the commentators who recapped the year—analysts and journalists shaking their heads in incredulous awe at the swift and dramatic changes of those twelve months—were proof enough that even the unflappable press corps found the year stunning in the momentous changes it brought. From the blitzkrieg "Mother of All Wars" in the Persian Gulf to the overnight disintegration of communism in the Soviet Union—1991 profoundly changed the face of world politics and power.

And with the advent of 1992, we might well have wondered what history could possibly do for an encore? Just ask the president of the United States, who attended an unforgettable state banquet in Tokyo as the new year dawned! Who's heart didn't go out to George Bush—a world leader who suddenly seemed very human and frail like the rest of us—as his intestinal flu and nausea were chronicled on global television?

This incident graphically revealed to us all—in a precarious flash—just how jittery international nerves have become. Thanks to modern communication, the world was instantly poised in apprehension for a few moments, waiting to learn the fate of the president. The near-panic in the press was again proof enough that with global nerves so much on edge, who knows what the immediate future might hold for us?

Regardless of what lies ahead, a far greater reality over-shadows the nightly summary of freshly exploding history on the evening news. For silently and unnoticed by the planet—and unreported by the press—a stealthy coalescing and secret marshaling of unseen forces is taking place. Forces whose agenda for this planet is to deceive and capture, to divide and conquer, to destroy and crush.

But is anybody watching? Is anybody ready?

In the pages just ahead, I'd like to invite you to join me in dusting off an ancient piece of apocalyptic literature—an old yellowed bit of prophetic parchment, in between the time-faded lines of which can still be seen gazing out the bloodshot eye of evil's last strategy—a strategy exposed in the searing light of "The Apocalypse of Jesus Christ," as the Greek reads for Revelation's opening line.

Apocalypse. Revelation. Because unless Jesus reveals the mystery of this dark midnight through which our planet is now passing, we shall never see the light of another day.

Let me be candid with you: What you are about to read may disturb you. The Apocalypse pulls very few punches. While Jesus intentionally and protectively cloaked His Apocalypse in cryptic symbols, the fact remains that He secreted there also enough internal keys to unlock the crim-son warnings of the Revelation. These blunt warnings were not written to win a place in Dale Carnegie's *How to Win Friends and Influence People.* But if Jesus does not warn His friends, then who will be ready for the most cataclysmic surprise ending of all time?

Somebody has got to read God's last warning, because somebody has got to be ready for history's last act. And *you* are the somebody whom the aged, weather-beaten disciple John must have had in mind when he penned his opening beatitude there on Patmos' rocky outcropping in the azure waters of the Aegean: "Blessed is the one who reads aloud the words of the prophecy, and blessed are those who hear and who keep what is written in it; for the time is near" (Revelation 1:3).

As the pastor of a university parish for the last nine years, I feel compelled to share with you what I now believe is fast becoming present truth for this world and for the church. The year 1991 forever crumbled the horizons of history. But beyond its time-strewn shards we can hear the tread of an approaching King. His opening beatitude promises a blessing for the journey.

Come then—let us voyage into the heart of the Apocalypse. For the time at last is here. We are truly standing "at the center of immensities, at the conflux of eternities."

Dwight K. Nelson
April, 1992
Pioneer Memorial Church
at Andrews University

Acknowledgments

As I wrote and preached my winter of 1992 sermon series on the Apocalypse at the Pioneer Memorial Church on the campus of Andrews University in southwestern Michigan, the conviction grew that this message must be shared beyond our university parish. I will always be grateful for my friends Edward and Verna Streeter, whose cheerful willingness and energetic skill helped prepare my sermon notes for editing and eventual publication.

I considered it more than coincidental that on the morning after a day of special prayer and fasting on this campus, I received a phone call from Dan Houghton of Hart Research Center at 5:30 a.m. his time. He'd been unable to sleep for two hours. Having heard something about our winter focus on the Apocalypse and its effect on our congregation, he inquired about the possibility of publishing the material. I'm excited about the formation of this new partnership with Hart Research Center.

To two friends and colleagues who were willing to

critique the manuscript and whose counsel and suggestions were invaluable, I will remain indebted. Raoul Dederen, professor of systematic theology at the Seventh-day Adventist Theological Seminary here at Andrews University, not only sat through the winter series, but also gave a portion of his spring break to read and edit the manuscript.

His constructive critique and perspective as a respected observer in ecumenical circles was a Godsend, as was his gracious willingness to counsel his former student and present pastor.

And Skip MacCarty, one of my staff colleagues, has shared the dream from the beginning and lent his kindred spirit in the journey. Late into the night and early in the morning, he has been there.

And to the parish that made this book possible—to the pastors and staff and members of the Pioneer Memorial Church: "I thank my God every time I remember you" (Philippians 1:3). Having embarked on this apocalyptic journey together, perhaps none of us will ever be quite the same again. But then, such is the transforming nature of the expectant hope of Christ's soon return—a day much closer now than when my journey with this congregation began nine years ago.

Last of all, I am most grateful of all for my wife Karen and our children Kirk and Kristin, whose companionship is a bright glow for me in the apocalyptic nightfall. Their patient willingness to let me be holed up at my keyboard for all those extra hours made this book possible. That we four journey together toward the finale is my greatest joy.

I wish to conclude this expression of gratitude with two words in Latin. A similar expression was designated recently as a motto of devotion to Mary the mother of Jesus: *Totus tuum*—"All Yours."

But as I read the Apocalypse and hear its clarion call for allegiance to Christ, the Lord and Lamb of Heaven, I have chosen to express the dedication of this book with the words *Solum tuus*—"Only Yours." For Christ is the only One Who can arouse this planet and prepare a people for His imminent return. "Only Yours" must define the devotion and dedication of an end-time generation that awaits Him.

Solum tuus, indeed, Lord Jesus.

REVELATION 12:7-12

And war broke out in heaven; Michael and his angels fought against the dragon. The dragon and his angels fought back, but they were defeated, and there was no longer any place for them in heaven.

The great dragon was thrown down, that ancient serpent, who is called the Devil and Satan, the deceiver of the whole world—he was thrown down to the earth, and his angels were thrown down with him.

Then I heard a loud voice in heaven, proclaiming, 'Now have come the salvation and the power and the kingdom of our God and the authority of his Messiah.

'For the accuser of our comrades has been thrown down, who accuses them day and night before our God.

'But they have conquered him by the blood of the Lamb and by the word of their testimony.

'For they did not cling to life even in the face of death.

'Rejoice then, you heavens and those who dwell in them! But woe to the earth and the sea.

'For the devil has come down to you with great wrath.'

1

How to Stalk a Dragon

Thomas Gillespie, dean of Princeton Theological Seminary, likes to tell the story of a schoolboy who was at his desk composing a report for his class. Needing an appropriate introduction, the boy headed for his mother, who was scurrying about the kitchen preparing the evening dinner. Without warning, he blurted, "Mother, how was I born?"

Mother had been expecting such a query regarding human reproduction from her boy, but she was hardly prepared to discuss the birds and the bees at this untimely moment. So she put him off with the old saw, "The stork brought you, dear."

The boy nodded and headed out to the livingroom, where his grandmother was knitting. Again with no warning, he questioned, "Grandma, how was my mother born?" But Grandma was from the Victorian era, and she wasn't about to touch this one with a ten-foot pole. So she, too, quickly explained, "My dear, the stork brought your mother."

"But Grandma," the boy persisted, "how were you born?"

"The stork brought me, too," was her neat and tidy answer.

Thanking her, the lad returned to his desk, picked up his pen, and began the report with these words: "There hasn't been a normal birth in our family for the last three generations."

And the boy is right, is he not? Come on, friend. There hasn't been a normal birth on this planet for years, has there? There hasn't been a normal birth even in the church for generations! Something's going on out there. Something's going on in here. The world and the church have changed. Dramatically and drastically changed.

A Desperate War

Because the fact of the matter is this: We are in a war, and the battle is intensifying. The strategy is contained in a single word: *intensification.*

Newspapers reported at the end of 1991 that there were fourteen wars waged across this planet that year, from Yugoslavia to Lithuania to Soweto to El Salvador to Iraq and Kuwait. Fourteen separate wars fought in 1991 between opposing human armies. Fourteen times the thousands of mothers and fathers who wept when their children didn't come marching home again. But in that list of fourteen, the war more human beings have fought and lost in than any other war in the history of civilization was not even mentioned.

The most costly battlefield, the most bloody war of all, is not even listed, because it's the one that occupies the space, not between two countries, but between two ears—yours and mine. It's the raging battle for the allegiance of every human mind and the loyalty of every human life.

There's a war going on, and the battle is intensifying.

Read them again—those cryptic words out of the heart of the Apocalypse: "And war broke out in heaven" (Revelation 12:7). If misery loves company, then you and I have company we love today, because before this war ever ruined your home and my heart, it devastated Someone else's.

"And war broke out in heaven." The astrophysicist Stephen Hawking has written a best seller you may have read—*A Brief History of Time*. Well, what you're about to read—in six terse verses—is the brief history of time from the divine perspective. It is the brief human history of a brutal cosmic war:

> And war broke out in heaven; Michael [the apocalyptic name for the preincarnate Christ] and his angels fought against the dragon. The dragon and his angels fought back, but they were defeated, and there was no longer any place for them in heaven. The great dragon was thrown down, that ancient serpent, who is called the Devil and Satan, the deceiver of the whole world—he was thrown down to the earth, and his angels were thrown down with him. Then I heard a loud voice in heaven proclaiming, 'Now have come the salvation and the power and the kingdom of our God and the authority of his Messiah, for the accuser of our comrades has been thrown down, who accuses them day and night before our God. But they have conquered him by the blood of the Lamb and by the word of their testimony, for they did not cling to life even in the face of death. Rejoice then, you heavens and those who dwell in them! But woe to the earth and the sea, for the devil has come down to you with great wrath, because he knows that his time is short!' (Revelation 12:7-12.)

Did you catch it? "Because he knows that his time is short!" Please note: Intensification is the name of the dragon's strategy. For his time and his intensity are inversely proportional, which simply means that the less he has of one, the more he has of the other. Which, being interpreted, means that with less and less time, the dragon has more and more rage. The closer we come to the end, the hotter his rage becomes.

Listen—we are in a war, and the battle is intensifying. For

that reason you will sometimes hear those in the older generations among us idealizing the tranquility and security of their childhood days and recalling how they were usually so much better behaved and certainly more mature than today's young. Then follow the bemoaning lamentations of how sad it is to see how kids today are turning out: exhibiting no respect for authority, dabbling in sexuality and substance abuse at increasingly earlier ages, rebelling, lying, and so on. And the implied query is, "Why can't they be like we were?"

Why Can't They Be Like We Were?

If you're part of an earlier generation, I'll tell you why: Because they don't live when you did. You bet it's worse today! There's a war going on, and the battle is intensifying. And our young are being decimated by an arsenal more sophisticated and destructive than that seen in any other age of history. They're getting shot up inside and outside of the church. "For the devil has come down to you with great wrath, because he knows that his time is short!"

Have you ever seen a counterfeit bill? I happen to carry a fake ten-dollar bill in my wallet. And if I ever handed the bill to you as legal tender, you'd spot the counterfeit as soon as you unfolded it. A friend in Oregon gave it to me years ago. It looks real when it's folded up. But open it, and you'll discover that it's only half as long as a genuine bill, and on the back side are printed the words: "Sorry, you've been ripped off, sucker." Not a very pleasing reminder, to be sure.

But for the sake of illustration, let's say that the original and genuine ten-dollar bill had been invented only yesterday. If I immediately set out to concoct and craft a counterfeit ten-dollar bill, then obviously any efforts on my part to copy the original would be based on a single day's worth of scrutiny and study.

But what if I had a week to craft my counterfeit? Doesn't it follow that with more time I would be able to devise a more "genuine" counterfeit? Which counterfeit bill would be more successful—the one based on a day's observation, or the one resulting from a week-long scrutiny? Obviously, the latter. What if I had a year to craft my counterfeit? What about a decade? A century? A millennium? Again, doesn't it logically follow that the longer I have to devise my counterfeit, the more highly deceptive and destructive it will be?

Enter now Lucifer—the dragon, the devil, Satan. Doesn't it follow that the generation living at the end of time will become the target of the most subtle and sophisticated, damning and deceptive counterfeits he has concocted over the course of his rebellion against his Creator and ours?

You bet it's worse today than when some of you grew up! It's a thousand-fold worse.

Because in his arsenal is a blitzkrieg of technological wonders that have hypnotized us today. Computer games subtly inculcate the values of violence and physical retaliation in the innocuous form of a portly old man named Mario, who wins his rewards by punching the daylights out of anyone or anything that gets in his way. And we eat it up!

Children's cartoons extol the values of the occult and the supernatural in such a gripping and tantalizing way you can't turn them off. And our kids are spellbound. (Literally, spell-bound!)

And for adult audiences, a variety of sitcoms and soaps mock the sanctity of marriage and belittle the responsibility of parenthood. Why, even Christians can laugh at the stuff for hours and somehow not feel the claws of a dragon rubbing their souls raw. A brilliant counterfeit strategy, really— one that subtly conditions viewers for the eventual and inevitable rainy day when they'll be faced with the same sexual temptation or ethical dilemma in real life. And in that moment of intensifying attack, they'll have been deceptively conditioned to meet the crisis in the very manner they've seen it met a hundred times in all those soaps. (Why, the very term "soaps" is a deception, since no one ever ends up cleansed by such vicarious arousal!)

And the dragon wins the battle again. And again. And again.

Every time I drive to a nearby town, I pass by a new establishment called Video Watch. A fine place, I'm sure, that makes its money renting home videos to anyone who'll pay a dollar or two. There's obviously nothing technologically or morally wrong with the medium of video in and of itself. (Our own congregation's "Perceptions" telecast, for example, shares the gospel coast to coast on the Three Angels' Broadcasting Network.)

But the dragon's behind-the-scenes strategy is to get people to sacrifice their values and discrimination. After all, it's only a Saturday night. Parents need to babysit their kids, right? (Or is it the other way around?) And what a simple solution: rent a video! So by the millions, they are brought into Christian homes—the claws of the dragon nowhere to be seen on their slick cover boxes. Never mind the rating. A dragon can often hide behind a G just as easily as behind an R.

It doesn't take a Ph.D. to figure out that for a counterfeit to work, it has to look a whole lot like the genuine. But if people pick up the counterfeit enough times, you can bank on the fact that they will soon lose their ability to discern between the false and the true. And when that happens, they become sitting ducks for the final deception.

I have the feeling that all of us, if we sat down for a quiet and pensive moment, could pretty much determine the strategy a smart dragon would use with anyone he wanted to bait: from TV programming, to magazine articles, to party life, to the quest for wealth and fame. Sure, you start with the good. And you rate it G. But then, as a thirst builds that seems to demand more and more in order to be slaked, you slowly and imperceptibly remove the genuine and replace it with the counterfeit, until in the end you have erected your own masterful falsehood in the throne room of their hearts. Brilliant. For a dragon.

But that's just it! He is no mythical dragon—this apocalyptic creature who rages and wages his warfare. We now know that we are up against a being who was once the most brilliant created mind in the universe (see Ezekiel 28). A being who can still transform himself into an angel of light (2 Corinthians 11:14). A being who tried to become God (see Isaiah 14). But heaven didn't have room for two Gods. So the one who arrived last left first. The usurper was cast out. But misery really does love company. And his last oath to God on the way out was, "I'll take every one of your children with me! Just you watch—just you wait!"

And when God became a man child (Revelation 12:5), just to prove that he meant what he said, the dragon impaled the incarnate Creator on a crimson stake. Then at last the witnessing universe knew the truth: that the heart and goal of a rebel is to destroy God Himself—to become God Himself. So demented is the dragon's dream that he has set out to obliterate anything or anyone that stands in the way of his black vision.

"Woe to the earth and the sea, for the devil has come down to you with great wrath, because he knows that his time is short!"

We are in a war, and the battle is intensifying.

So How Shall We Survive?

So how then shall we survive, you and I? How shall we live the months that remain to us? "But they have conquered him by the blood of the Lamb and by the word of their testimony, for they did not cling to life even in the face of death" (Revelation 12:11).

Isn't it clearly evident that to survive the dragon's intensifying onslaught, we are going to have to cling to a power outside ourselves? The dragon is too pervasive; he is everywhere. And he isn't sleeping on his watch.

I spent a few hours in Amsterdam a few weeks ago with a day layover on my way to South Africa. What a sad exhibit that city is—as are our most of our urban centers—of the harvest of liberated morality and freedom from religious mores. All I wanted was a postcard to send home to the family. But strolling down the crowded boulevard of that main thoroughfare, all I could find were postcard racks placed out on the sidewalks for the tourists—racks filled with what in this country we'd call pornographic cards. Not subtle, but blatant and overt. And nobody blinks an eye! The dragon is that pervasive. His wares are on display not just for "dirty old men," but for young, vibrant lives just blossoming into adulthood. I have 3,000 such lives in my own parish. Sitting ducks for a furious dragon. But then, aren't we all?

He certainly was—the God who infiltrated this bastion of evil. Bethlehem's Babe. "The rightful King," as C. S. Lewis put it, who "landed in disguise." Cloaked in human garb like one of us, He was "God with us." He ate with us and slept with us; He laughed with us and wept with us. And then suddenly, brutally, He died for us. The Lamb of the Apocalypse was slain by Lucifer. And when Jesus rent the awful darkness of Golgotha with that piercing scream, "My God, my God, why have you forsaken me?" we knew at last the infinite price of this bloody war. And when His battered head raised up in that pent-up death cry, "It is finished!" then began to clang the triumphant death knell of the dragon's kingdom—a wild pealing that still resounds across the canyons and chasms of God's universe.

> Now have come the salvation and the power and the kingdom of our God and the authority of his Messiah, for the accuser of our comrades has been thrown down (Revelation 12:10).

Listen to how another apocalyptic classic, *The Great Controversy*, puts it:

> In the banishment of Satan from heaven, God declared His justice and maintained the honor of His throne. But when man sinned through yielding to the deceptions of this apostate spirit, God gave an evidence of His love by yielding up His only-begotten Son to die for the fallen race. In the atonement the character of God is revealed. The mighty argument of the cross demonstrates to the whole

universe that the course of sin which Lucifer had chosen was in no wise chargeable upon the government of God (p. 501).

In the Saviour's expiring cry, "It is finished," the death knell of Satan was rung. The great controversy which had been so long in progress was then decided, and the final eradication of evil was made certain (p. 503).

I was preaching a few days ago in Sacramento, California. The Friday evening meeting was soon to begin, when I spotted him walking down the center aisle of the church—a young man with a black T-shirt on, and across his shirt in bright red letters the name SATAN. I did a quick double-take. No question about it. There they were in big red letters: "SATAN." I hurriedly began to wonder what sort of crowd and meeting this was going to be. Then he moved closer and extended his hand for a handshake, and I could read the small print below in white letters: ". . . is defeated." Whew! I was still among friends!

The triumphant news of the Apocalypse for friend and foe is just that: "Satan is defeated." For that indeed was Calvary's victorious shout on what became a very Good Friday long ago. The Lamb had conquered the dragon. And every follower of Jesus was henceforth assured that same crimson victory! "They have conquered him by the blood of the Lamb" (Revelation 12:11).

How to stalk a dragon? By the blood of the Lamb. Which is why the twelfth chapter of the Apocalypse ends with a portrait of an end-time people in love with Jesus:

Then the dragon was angry with the woman, and went off to make war on the rest of her children, those who keep the commandments of God and hold the testimony of Jesus (Revelation 12:17).

And by the way, it's no accident that Revelation 14:12

sounds just like Revelation 12:17, since both texts portray the same end-time generation: "Here is a call for the endurance of the saints, those who keep the commandments of God and hold fast to the faith of Jesus." Both verses describe a people who hold on to Jesus.

And therein lies their secret. For, you see, there is a double intensification going on at the end of time: *A dragon who intensifies his force is met by a generation that intensifies its faith.* Intensified force calls for intensified faith, for in the end there is a head-on cosmic clash of the dragon and the last generation.

I believe that now is the time for that generation to arise. How are they described? They are the ones holding on to Jesus. But how shall I hold on? you ask. Finally, consider some lines from *The Great Controversy* :

> We are living in the most solemn period of this world's history. The destiny of earth's teeming multitudes is about to be decided. Our own future wellbeing and also the salvation of other souls depend upon the course which we now pursue. We need to be guided by the Spirit of truth. Every follower of Christ should earnestly inquire: "Lord, what wilt Thou have me to do?" (p. 601)

And with that admonition comes an intensely specific how-to piece of counsel for Jesus' end-time generation:

> We need to humble ourselves before the Lord, with fasting and prayer, and to meditate much upon His word. We should now seek a deep and living experience in the things of God. We have not a moment to lose. Events of vital importance are taking place around us. Sleep not, sentinels of God; the foe is lurking near, ready at any moment, should you become lax and drowsy, to spring upon you and make you his prey (*Ibid.*).

Did you catch that? "With fasting and prayer, meditate much upon His word." You see, *the intensification of force must be met by the intensification of faith.* I know you've prayed before; I know you've read from the Scriptures before. But can you see and sense that in this intensifying warfare of life—a battle called the Great Controversy—the Apocalypse is summoning you and me to a new intensifying of faith? So while you and I may have enjoyed the semblance of a devotional life in the past, the time has come in this battle for us to intensify our search to know the mind and heart of God. The stakes are eternal; it's rapidly becoming a matter of life and death.

In the face of the intensifying battle raging around us, is this not the time to turn over a new leaf, to write a new chapter, to begin a new kind of prayer and study life with God? No fancy gimmicks. Just some old-fashioned intensity that hasn't been very popular in our circles for a long, long time. To take hold of Jesus . . . to discover a new dimension of power in our relationship with God: it's time, my friend.

A young school boy was racing for the bus one morning. Panting and gasping for air, he arrived at the bus stop just in time to see the bus vanish down the road. A bystander who witnessed it remarked, "Too bad, son. You just didn't run fast enough." To which the honest boy gulped back: "No sir, I ran fast enough; I just didn't start soon enough."

We're running out of time. The dragon knows it. I know you can run fast enough. The question is, will you start soon enough? Don't put it off. There's a war going on, and the battle is intensifying. You can't afford a late start. Which makes right now the right time to make the right start. "They have conquered him by the blood of the Lamb and by the word of their testimony." It can be your testimony, too.

REVELATION 13:1-10

Then the dragon took his stand on the sand of the seashore. And I saw a beast rising out of the sea; and on its horns were ten diadems, and on it heads were blasphemous names. And the beast that I saw was like a leopard, its feet were like a bear's, and its mouth like a lion's mouth. And the dragon gave it his power and his throne and great authority.

One of its heads seemed to have received a death-blow, but its mortal wound had been healed. In amazement the whole earth followed the beast. They worshiped the dragon, for he had given his authority to the beast, and they worshiped the beast, saying, "Who is like the beast, and who can fight against it?"

The beast was given a mouth uttering haughty and blasphemous words, and it was allowed to exercise authority for forty-two months.

It opened its mouth to utter blasphemies against God, blaspheming his name and his dwelling, that is, those who dwell in heaven.

Also it was allowed to make war on the saints and to conquer them. It was given authority over every tribe and people and language and nation, and all the inhabitants of the earth will worship it, everyone whose name has not been written from the foundation of the world in the book of life of the Lamb that was slaughtered.

If you are to be taken captive, into captivity you go; if you kill with the sword, with the sword you must be killed. Here is a call for the endurance and faith of the saints.

2

Beauty and the Beast

Her story is one of those unbelievable tales that deserves to go straight into Paul Harvey's *The Rest of the Story* collection! (And if not Paul Harvey's, then at least Ripley's *Believe It or Not!*)

Her name—Evelyn Glennie. Her age—26. Her profession—percussion virtuoso—graduate with honors from London's prestigious Royal Academy of Music. From there she embarked on a professional career her doctors said was impossible. For Evelyn beats, shakes, rattles, or squeezes more than 600 musical instruments, as the world's only full-time percussion soloist (from drums to marimbas, from xylophones to cymbals, from tympani to tambourines).

And this young woman who speaks with a lilting Scottish accent and who has been blessed with perfect musical pitch is making history! For she gave the first solo percussion recital in the 95-year history of the BBC's Prom Concerts at

Royal Albert Hall. And in November of 1991 she scored another first, as this daughter of a Scottish farmer debuted in the Kennedy Center in Washington, D.C. .

Her debut with the Los Angeles Philharmonic at the Hollywood Bowl was also a smashing success. But the wild applause from her appreciative concert audience fell on deaf ears. For Evelyn Glennie is deaf. She plays 600 instruments without hearing them! Impossible?

Here's how she's made the impossible possible. Evelyn Glennie has learned to play her concert percussion solos by the subtle vibrations of tone and pitch that she feels in her body. Which is why she usually kicks off her shoes during a performance, to sense the reverberations from the wooden stage.

You see, she began to go deaf at the age of eight, and by twelve it was permanent. They said it couldn't be done. But they forgot to convince Evelyn, who would stand outside the wall of the music room as her teacher struck various notes, to discover where the notes tingled or vibrated in her fingers or wrists. She now learns entire scores of complex music by playing a tape recorder between her knees. What do you suppose she entitled her recent autobiography? *Good Vibrations*. I like that!

Isn't it phenomenal? She doesn't hear a word—but she can feel the vibrations. I wonder: Is she a parable of the world? A world that can't hear the Word, but feels and senses deep within its earthy soul the vibrations of an impending conflict?

In this *Countdown to the Showdown* we return to some ancient apocalyptic prophecies whose words are hardly heard, let alone listened to, anymore. But even if you can't hear their words, surely today you can feel their vibrations— the vibrations and reverberations of a prophetic word at last coming true. Which is more than true for "Beauty and the Beast." For the beast has come again.

The Beast

A couple of his birthdays ago, we took our son, Kirk, and a few of his buddies down to the Studebaker Museum in South

Bend, Indiana, for a trip into a surrealistic world of ancient beasts. Through carefully staged lighting and sound, these massive rubber-skinned prehistoric creatures twisted and twitched, snarled and snapped with blood-curdling roars. And all of it before our very eyes! Though we kept telling ourselves they were all electronically controlled, lifeless manikins, believe me when I confess that they looked and sounded frighteningly alive and utterly ferocious!

Imagine how the aged disciple John must have reacted as, in horror, he saw in vision an amalgamated beast dripping with the brine of the wind-swept sea stalking toward him: "And I saw a beast rising out of the sea, having ten horns and seven heads; and on its horns were ten diadems, and on its heads were blasphemous names. And the beast that I saw was like a leopard, its feet were like a bear's, and its mouth was like a lion's mouth. And the dragon gave it his power and his throne and great authority" (Revelation 13:1, 2).

Spotted like a leopard, the beast possessed the raking claws of a grizzly bear and the tearing fangs of a lion, had seven heads and ten horns, and was dripping with water. What on earth is this amalgamation?

"And on its head were blasphemous names." Remember what blasphemy is? You're right. It's taking the name of God in vain. And did my parents ever drill that one into me when I was a boy! I grew up in Japan, and when I was four my family came back to the States on furlough. And while we were visiting in Oshawa, Canada, where my Grandpa and Grandma Nelson were working, I remember watching Timmy and Lassie on television. And because Timmy was always saying "Gosh" and "Gee Whiz," I figured I could, too. Whereupon, in an irrefutable way, my parents taught me that those two slang words were abbreviated expletives for Jesus (Gee) and God (Gosh). And so it was, "No more, do you understand?" And I came to understand rather quickly! But then, no parent wants his child to blaspheme.

Actually the Greek word here in the Apocalypse is *blasphemia*, from which our English word *blaspheme* is a direct transliteration or copy. But notice how the dictionary expands its definition: "Impious or profane speaking of God, or of sacred persons or things." And then the dictionary adds this theological twist to blasphemy: "The act of claiming the attributes of God."

So whatever else this beast power is, it is a power that, among other characteristics, claims the attributes and prerogatives of God. But that's not all. Read on:

> One of its heads seemed to have received a death-blow, but its mortal wound had been healed. In amazement the whole earth followed the beast. They worshiped the dragon, for he had given his authority to the beast, and they worshiped the beast, saying, "Who is like the beast, and who can fight against it?"
>
> The beast was given a mouth uttering haughty and blasphemous words, and it was allowed to exercise authority for forty-two months. It opened its mouth to utter blasphemies against God, blaspheming his name and his dwelling, that is, those who dwell in heaven. Also it was allowed to make war on the saints and to conquer them. It was given authority over every tribe and people and language and nation, and all the inhabitants of the earth will worship it, everyone whose name has not been written from the foundation of the world in the book of life of the Lamb that was slaughtered (Revelation 13:3-8).

Did you catch the length of its domination? Forty-two months. Which calculates into three and a half years, or 1,260 days. But to what kind of time period could this possibly be referring? Interestingly, from the time of the Christian writer Tichonius in the late fourth century onward, various Bible scholars have consistently embraced the biblical key for symbolic time prophecies, namely, that a day represents a year (based on God's usage of that "time key" in Ezekiel 4:6 and Numbers 14:34).

So what John is being shown here in this dripping wet, amalgamated beast is the symbol of a power that would hold sway in the history of the Christian church (which is what the Apocalypse, of course, is all about—a graphic symbolizing of the church's history from the cross of Jesus on through to His return to Earth the second time). This power, therefore, would dominate church history for 1,260 years. But who—or what—is this beast power?

Working strictly with the internal evidence of this prophecy, what do we know about this beast power? First of all, from even a cursory reading of the prophecy, the beast clearly represents *a religious power*. For only a religious institution would receive the worship of the world (as it does in verse 8), seeking to usurp the place and worship of God. Secondly, it is also clear that the beast represents *a political power.* For only a political power has a throne and crowns and a global dominion (verses 1 and 2). But thirdly, it is a religio-political power that holds *global* sway. And so it is fair—and even essential—to consider this beast power a *geo-religio-political* institution.

But there's more. For the prophecy reveals that this geo-religio-political power that would hold sway for over a millennium in history becomes wounded in the prophecy (verse 3)—that is, it is nearly destroyed. But amazingly, that wound heals. Then, after the healing, this power reasserts its global dominance. And finally, this power is depicted as making war on the people of God (verse 7).

So what do we have? A geo-religio-political power that (1) is dominant for over 1,200 years in the history of Christianity and then (2) is unexpectedly and mysteriously wounded, but that (3) is eventually healed of its wound and (4) finally holds global sway.

The Beauty

Before we conclude identifying this power, I must share with you what you may have never before seen in this passage: This beast is an intentional counterfeit of the

Lamb of the Apocalypse. For if you look carefully, you will discover seven parallels between the beast and the Lamb. And who is the Lamb? Revelation 5:6 leaves no doubt as to who this apocalyptic symbol represents when it describes "a Lamb standing [beside God's throne] as if it had been slaughtered, having seven horns and seven eyes."

Those around the throne sing a paean to the Lamb that includes the glad exclamation, "You are worthy . . . for you were slaughtered and by your blood you ransomed for God saints from every tribe and language and people and nation" (verse 9). The Lamb is the apocalyptic symbol for our crucified, resurrected, and ascended Lord Jesus. Notice now the startling parallels between the Lamb and the beast:

1. Both the Lamb and the beast arise out of water as they begin their influence on earth: One out of the Jordan River at His baptism; the other out of the apocalyptic sea.

2. Both the Lamb and the beast exercise power for three and a half years: One for three and a half literal years, as it was for Jesus in His ministry on earth; and the other for a prophetic or symbolic three and a half years (1,260 days/years).

3. Both the Lamb and the beast are mortally wounded; in fact, the Greek word describing the beast's "death blow" in Revelation 13:3 is identical to the word for the Lamb's being "slaughtered" in Revelation 5:6 and 13:8.

4. Both the Lamb and the beast come back to life (see Revelation 1:18 and 13:3).

5. Both the Lamb and the beast have horns: the Lamb has seven horns (Revelation 5:6); the beast ten (Revelation 13:1).

6. Both of them receive honor and worship, to which only One of them is entitled. (Interestingly, the language of global worship for the beast in Revelation 13:4 is the same language ascribed to divine worship in Exodus 15:11 and Psalm 35:10!)

7. And finally, both the Lamb and the beast seek to reach every nation, kindred, tongue, and people (14:6 and 13:7).

Look at them carefully. Seven incontrovertible parallels between the Lamb and the beast—Beauty and the beast. Seven parallels that powerfully portray the reality that somebody is trying very hard to be like the Lamb—to look like the Lamb! Somebody is trying desperately to take Christ's place. In fact, the Greek word *anti* means "instead of." So *anti*-Christ means "instead of Christ."

Somebody is secretly trying to take the place of Jesus. A somebody who has had his proud eye on the position of the Son of God from the beginning of the rebellion called the Great Controversy. A somebody who started a war in heaven and has vowed to keep it raging on earth. Lucifer the dragon against Christ the Lamb. Revelation 13 is the struggle between the Lamb and Lucifer, between Beauty and the beast. So desperate is Lucifer that he creates in the history of the Christian church a counterfeit for himself through the existence of this beast—a counterfeit intended to look just like Jesus!

Before we identify this beast power by name, I must share this caveat—this warning disclaimer: Never forget that the Apocalypse is describing a power and not a person or a people, an institution and not an individual, a system and not a soul.

On the basis of this prophecy, nobody has the right to point to a neighbor or a friend or a colleague or an acquaintance and say: "Ah, you must be what this is all about." Never! The Lamb Himself said, "Judge not, that you be not judged." For it could be that in the end the very sin of Lucifer that brought him down could bring your own soul down—the dark sin of pride and self-worship.

But Who Is the Beast?

In my library, I have a set of books by Leroy Froom called *The Prophetic Faith of Our Fathers* that traces how the Apocalypse has been interpreted over the history of the Christian church—a four-volume compendium that Dr. Wilbur M. Smith of Fuller Theological Seminary commended as being unparalleled "for exhaustiveness, freshness, and dependability in our language."

I'm amazed, as I study these books, both by the number and by the unanimity of those Christian writers and Bible students over the dusty span of the church's history who agree as to who this geo-religio-political power really is. In fact, you may go all the way back to Eberhard II, the archbishop of Salzburg (A.D. 1200-1246), to discover a long line of scholars who believed and taught that this beast power of the Apocalypse (as well as of Daniel) is the institution of the papacy of Rome.

And as soon as one concludes that this beast power of Revelation 13 symbolizes the Church of Rome, I realize how easy it is to declare such a conviction nothing more than stereotypical Protestantism—an archaic appendage to medieval thinking. (Incidentally, the Apocalypse offers a warning to stereotypical Protestantism as well, which we'll consider in the next chapter.)

After all, the 1,260 years of the Dark and Middle Ages are past. The world is enlightened now, and previous barbarities are no longer relevant.

So what if in A.D. 538 the barbarian seige of Rome was broken, thus elevating the Bishop of Rome to the position of preeminent leader within the Catholic Church—and so what if 1260 years later in A.D. 1798, the papacy was mortally wounded when the pope was taken prisoner and died in exile?)* So what if during Garibaldi's revolution in Italy

---

*The City of Rome was beseiged in A.D. 538 by a barbarian nation—the Ostrogoths. To aid the cause of Catholics in the West, Justinian—the emperor who ruled the Eastern half of the Roman Empire from Constantinople—dispatched an army that year that broke the seige and liberated the city. As a result, the emperor enabled the Church in Rome to claim the preeminence that he decreed in A.D. 533 in his 131st Novella (New Constitution): "Hence, in accordance with the provisions of these Councils, we order that the Most Holy Pope of ancient Rome shall hold the first rank of all the Pontiffs, but the Most Blessed Archbishop of Constantinople, or New Rome, shall occupy the second place after the Holy Apostolic See of ancient Rome, which shall take precedence over all other sees." Her unrivaled precedence was mortally wounded 1,260 years later when Napoleon's General Berthier, at the head of a French army, entered Rome in 1798, proclaimed the papal political rule at an end, and exiled Pope Pius VI to France, where he died a political prisoner.

(1866-70) the Roman Church was stripped of even her lands, leaving the pope a virtual prisoner in the Vatican? And so what if fifty-nine years later, on February 11, 1929, an Italian leader named Mussolini signed a concordat with Cardinal Gaspari that restored a portion of those lands, thus ushering the papacy once again into international status by granting it geo-political power? So the wound was healed. So what?

No, the question is not, So what? The question needs to be, So what's next? Any reader of this apocalyptic prophecy cannot escape the throbbing prediction of a yet-to-be global dominance by this same power, that will in turn climax human history. It can hardly be a stereotypical Protestant response to wonder how this divine prophecy is yet to unfold.

Clearly, in this portion of the Apocalypse, the Church of Rome is front and center. The internal evidence of the thirteenth chapter that identifies it cannot be summarily dismissed. This prophetic description of a geo-religio-political power that has held dominance for over a millennium of church history must not be hastily ignored. Nor should the apocalyptic prediction that this very institution will one day exercise unprecedented global sway at the end of time.

Is the Wound Healed?

> One of the beast's heads seemed to have received a death-blow, but its mortal wound had been healed. In amazement, the whole earth followed the beast. They worshiped the dragon, for he had given his authority to the beast, and they worshiped the beast, saying, "Who is like the beast and who can fight against it?" And all the inhabitants of the earth will worship it, everyone whose name has not been written from the foundation of the world in the book of life of the Lamb that was slaughtered (Revelation 13:3, 4, 8).

On January 11, 1992, diplomats representing over a hundred nations gathered in the "sumptuous frescoed Royal

Hall of the Vatican," as the Associated Press release put it, to hear "the pope's major foreign policy statement of the year," as John Paul II gave his annual New Year's address to all the "diplomats accredited to the Holy See" (*South Bend Tribune*, January 12, 1992). Over 100 nations sent their diplomats to hear what Pope John Paul II would have to say about 1992. But then, is anybody surprised? By early 1990, John Paul had visited, since his coronation in 1978, more than 90 nations and had given 1,559 speeches in 32 languages, being seen or heard— either in the flesh or via audio-video circuits—by 3.5 billion people. Was anybody really surprised? Who would possibly challenge the geo-political ascendancy of Rome anymore?

Note how *Foreign Policy*, a journal published for the diplomatic corps, put it in an article in the Spring issue for 1990 entitled, "Papal Foreign Policy." Written by J. Bryan Hehir, professor of ethics and international politics at Georgetown University's School of Foreign Service and a counselor for social policy for the United States Catholic Conference, the article describes what he calls "the most activist papacy in modern history." In fact, "Not since the Middle Ages can a comparably broad conception of papal activity be found" (p. 27).

Did you catch that? "Not since the Middle Ages" the author writes. Which is precisely what the Apocalypse declares about this Middle Ages power whose mortal wound will be healed in the end: It will regain and exercise its previous power.

Hehir further observes: "The Vatican acts like a state but not simply a state" (p. 47). But it is "its capacity to act like a church and a state" that creates a "paradox in this papacy. [For] the pope has established himself as a major figure in world affairs. But he consistently denies any political interest" (pp. 36, 37). Such denial notwithstanding, Hehir notes that "John Paul II's role, especially but not only in Eastern Europe, has been a political event of vast proportions" (p. 36).

So who was surprised when Boris Yeltsin recently hurried to Rome on one of his first visits outside the new Commonwealth? Both political science and ancient prophecy offer a clear and certain explanation for such evident ascendancy on the part of Rome today. "Clearly, there is great potential for a repositioned Catholicism, led by a philosopher-pope with an acute sense of geopolitical trends, to play an activist role in both the East-West and North-South agendas of the 1990s" (p. 48).

North, south, east, and west. "In amazement the whole earth followed the beast" (Revelation 13:3).

Listen to Pope John Paul II, on October 28, 1978, as he addressed the world at his papal coronation, speaking successively in ten languages: "Open wide the doors of Christ. To his saving power open the boundaries of states, economic and political systems, the vast fields of culture and civilization and development. Do not be afraid . . . I want your support in this, my mission" (Malachi Martin, *The Keys of This Blood*, Simon and Schuster, New York, 1990, p. 63).

Malachi Martin, a Catholic scholar and author who cannot be suspected of liberal views, would later extol "the divine claim he [Pope John Paul II] did indeed have to exercise spiritual authority and moral primacy over all those who wield such temporal power in our lives" (*Ibid.*). Which is why Martin, the once-Jesuit and still-loyal advocate of the papacy, can describe John Paul in his revealing book as possessing "the unrivaled personal status as the most visible and well-known human being of the twentieth century" (p. 123). "The Holy Father," Martin writes, "was making his very own a truly central spot on the world stage."

Listen to the more than coincidental resemblance between the geo-religio-political power described by the Apocalypse and Malachi Martin's firm contention:

> The most important facts and details about the Roman Church from the point of view of any secular power holder, however, all come down to one point. There is a tacit agreement among the great international political and financial leaders that the very attributes that give the Holy See its geo-religious

power and capability provide it, as well, with everything essential for the same power and capability
on the political plane. In secular eyes, the Roman
Church stands alone in every practical sense as the
first, fully realized, fully practicing and totally independent geo-political force in the current world
arena. And the Pope is by definition the world's
first fully fledged geo-political leader (p. 143).

Having heard from a well-known voice within conservative Catholicism, how would a liberal voice within the Roman Church speak? Penny Lernoux was the Latin American
Affairs correspondent for the *National Catholic Reporter*. An
award-winning journalist, she wrote the book *People of God:
The Struggle for World Catholicism*, which was published in
1989, the year of her death at 49. As a liberal Catholic journalist, Lernoux makes an impassioned appeal for the papacy
to abandon what she describes as its growing authoritarian
and hierarchical power that calls Roman Catholics to conform to Rome's decrees. "John Paul's Vatican longs for the
past; the pope wishes to restore an authoritarian church
model based on that of the Middle Ages, when the state and
its institutions were uniformly Catholic" (Penguin Books,
New York, 1989, p. 11).

Once again we find the more than coincidental observation that Rome is returning to her Middle Ages *modus operandi*. Once more from a Catholic pen, we encounter the
annotation of Rome's evident quest for her Middle Ages
global power base.

Listen to Mikhail Gorbachev, former president of the Soviet
Union and now a nationally syndicated columnist here in the
United States. In a March 9, 1992 article in the *South Bend Tribune*
entitled "Pope Played Major Role in Reforms," Gorbachev
discloses: "I have carried on an intensive correspondence with
Pope John Paul II since we met at the Vatican in December 1989.
And I think ours will be an ongoing dialogue."

The former president went on to declare: "Personally, I
would be glad to take any opportunity to continue working

with the pope, and I am certain that this desire is mutual and will prove lasting." What role does Gorbachev envision for John Paul in the future? "I am certain that the actions undertaken by John Paul II are of immense significance." And then he predicts: "Pope John Paul II will play an enormous political role now that profound changes have occurred in European history." The former head of communism (political atheism) hails the leadership of Rome!

Say what you will about John Paul II, his peripatetic global ministry has raised his papal office to a height never before witnessed in the history of Christendom. Billy Graham, Ronald Reagan, George Bush, Mikhail Gorbechev (who called him the "world's highest moral authority"), the Dalai Lama, the Archbishop of Canterbury, Boris Yeltsin, Robert Schuller, and a host of religious and political leaders have all sought their private audiences with the Holy See.

"In amazement the whole earth followed."

The recently retired Archbishop of Canterbury, Robert Runcie, leader of the 70 million Anglicans in the world, stepping out from his audience with John Paul, addressed the congregation in the Church of St. Gregory: "For the universal church, I renew the plea. Could not all Christians come to reconsider the kind of primacy the bishop of Rome exercised within the early church, a 'presiding of love' for the sake of the unity of the churches in the diversity of their mission?" (*South Bend Tribune*, October 1, 1989.)

Consider the following incident as related in the September, 1989, issue of *Ecumenical Trends*, which reported on Pope John Paul II's visit to five Scandinavian countries in June, 1989. In one country the pope was conducting a Roman mass. At the end of the line were two Lutheran bishops, who approached him. One bishop spoke: "I am sorry we cannot go to the same table, but I am here as a symbol of our common longing for unity." The account ended with these words: "The pope then blessed the two bishops."

Are the calls for unity with Rome being heeded? I went through the last two years' worth of the monthly *Ecumenical*

Trends magazine. In these issues I read of the following dialogues for unity and reunion taking place in Christendom: Talks between the Roman Catholic Church and Eastern Orthodoxy; between the Roman Church and Methodists; between Rome and the Jews; between the Roman Catholic Church and the Anglican Church; between Rome and the Lutherans; even between the Roman Church and Southern Baptists (who have had a "Scholar's Dialogue" between their two communions that has met eighteen times over the last few years).

And who do you suppose will make the necessary accommodations to achieve this sought-after unity? Note carefully the Vatican's answer, reported in the December 16, 1991, issue of *Time* magazine. At the conclusion of recent talks between Rome and the Anglican Church, the Vatican issued a statement. And *Time* commented on "the Holy See's official 12-page response" with this observation:

> Rather than endorse the painstakingly crafted agreement, the Vatican issued a statement insisting that a reunited church must be built upon a papacy that is a God-given, "permanent" institution with "universal" jurisdiction, "directly founded" by Jesus Christ. The text also reasserts the pope's personal power to teach infallibly on faith and morals.

Yes, Rome seeks unity. But the Vatican has made it more than apparent at whose expense that unity must be achieved.

And yet the movement to unite goes on. Consider this report made by the *Catholic Herald* in its October 11, 1991, edition. The front-page headline reads: "John Paul in historic unity meeting."

> For the first time since the Reformation, the Pope prayed at the tomb of St. Peter under the Vatican basilica with two Lutheran bishops this week, as part of a series of milestone events for ecumenism. . . . Pope John Paul II told the congregation of politicians, diplomats and both Catholic and

Protestant hierarchy that the "centuries-long mis-
trust between Catholics and Lutherans has dis-
solved" making way for "more tangible faith and
hope." . . . In his address, Sweden's Lutheran
Bishop Bertil Werkstrom stressed that the Protestant reformation was never intended to forge a rift
between the Christian community. "It was meant
as a movement for reform within the one, holy apostolic church . . . . The moment has come when we
must say that the denunciations at the time of the
reformation are no longer valid," he said.

"The denunciations [of Martin Luther] at the time of the
reformation are no longer valid"? Let those who have ears hear!

And lest you conclude that the apocalyptic interpretation
that you have read in this chapter is peculiar to me or to my
church, consider the latest book from well-known evangelical
author David Hunt. In *Global Peace,* Hunt unabashedly links the
Roman Church with the antichrist of prophecy. Referring to the
global adulation the pope has been receiving, Hunt warns that
"the church and 'Christianity' of ancient Rome are being resurrected before our very eyes with the blessing of the world's
religions and leading Protestants as well."

Hunt candidly observes:

The fact that Catholicism is taking over from Communism is hardly cause for rejoicing; it is a strategic
and necessary move. The Roman empire cannot be
revived without Catholicism recovering its dominant role. That recovery is now taking place with
the support of Protestant leaders.

"In amazement the whole earth followed the beast."

What Does All This Mean?

So what does all of this mean for you and me? In the
shadows of this thirteenth chapter, I hear four clarion calls to
this planet. First, I hear the call of Jesus: "Now when these

things begin to take place, stand up and raise your heads, because your redemption is drawing near" (Luke 21:28). My friend, I believe that in the phenomenal resurgence and ascendancy of the Church of Rome, we are witnessing today a fulfillment of apocalyptic prophecy. There is a mysterious confluence and convergence of global factors that must draw our minds and souls back to God's communication here in Revelation 13.

But it is not a time for fear; it is an hour for faith. For on the heels of this end-time resurgence comes the greatest good news of all: Jesus will soon return!

Second, in this apocalyptic prophecy I hear the call of God to honest-hearted Roman Catholics all over this planet. I must affirm it again: While God warns of the institution, He wants the individual. Just a few chapters later you will hear His apocalyptic cry to them, "Come out of her, My people" (Revelation 18:4). They are His people, every single one of them. We are all God's people. Penny Lernoux's title—*People of God*—is right! Which is why in the end God is so urgent in summoning humanity to turn from false gods and counterfeit institutions, to come back to the Creator God and Father of us all.

There is growing discontent in Roman Catholicism today. The liberals despair of a church that, with iron authority, would command their consciences. The conservatives despair of a church that would barter away the truth of God. And so to my Roman Catholic friends who are reading this, I would quietly appeal: Turn your heart toward the One who still declares, "I am the way, and the truth, and the life" (John 14:6). Jesus is calling you and me to a radical commitment to the truth in His Word.

For that very reason I hear a third summons in this apocalyptic prophecy. It is the call of Jesus to my own church—the church I love. A divine summons to quickly possess the window of opportunity that remains open on this planet. The messages of the Three Angels in Revelation 14 must go quickly to all the world. Globally and locally, the church must seize the opportunities granted by this brief respite between headlines. We must tell what we have discovered in this Book about God. It is not our message; it is God's message and His mission that must be shared from door to door and heart to heart.

But there is a fourth and final call that I hear in this prophecy. And that is God's summons to choose this day between the Lamb and Lucifer, between the Beauty and the beast. Ultimately that is the final choice left to every man and woman and child on this planet. Whom will you serve? If the Lamb is God, serve Him; if Lucifer is God, then serve him. But how long will you go limping between two masters?

No wonder this prophecy ends with the summons: "Here is a call for the endurance and faith of the saints" (Revelation 13:10). In the face of intensifying force, here is a call for intensifying faith.

"Here I Stand"

You will not be the first to stand. Let me close by reminding you of one who long ago stood all alone against the religio-political power of the Middle Ages church. His name? Martin Luther.

The night before he was to return to the Diet (or council) of Worms and defend his writings and faith in the Scriptures, Luther suffered what we would call today a panic attack. Gripped by the icy paralysis of crippling fear, he crumbled to the floor of his tiny room that dark hour in Worms. His anguished face pressed against the earth, Luther's sobs rend the black night.

The great Reformation historian D'Aubigné recounted those cries: "'O God, do Thou help me against all the wisdom of the world. Do this, . . . Thou alone; . . . for this is not my work, but Thine. . . . O Lord, help me! Faithful and unchangeable God, in no man do I place my trust. . . . Thou hast chosen me for this work. . . . Stand at my side, for the sake of Thy well-beloved Jesus Christ, who is my defense, my shield, and my strong tower'" (*History of the Reformation of the Sixteenth Century*, p. 259).

Through that long midnight hour he poured out his soul to his Lord. And when the day dawned, it arose upon a man whose worn knees and clinging faith had laid hold upon the Divine. Finally ushered back into the judicial chambers of that Diet, Luther stood now before the greatest living personages of church and state. Without trace of fear or embarrassment, this young Augustinian pastor and professor launched into a grueling defense of his faith in the Holy Scriptures and of his humble efforts to publish the truth he had discovered therein.

Exhausted, he finished at last his lonely defense, only to have the magistrates call him to repeat all his words, this time in Latin. So it was that Providence ordained a twin defense that fated day in court, first in German and then in Latin. When, at the end of the wearying day, Luther was once more grilled, "Will you, or will you not, retract?" he calmly replied: "'Since your most serene majesty and your high mightinesses require from me a clear, simple, and precise answer, I will give you one, and it is this: I cannot submit my faith either to the pope or to the councils, because it is clear as the day that they have frequently erred and contradicted each other. Unless therefore I am convinced by the testimony of Scripture or by the clearest reasoning—unless I am persuaded by means of the passages I have quoted, and unless they thus render my conscience bound by the word of God, *I cannot and I will not retract,* for it is unsafe for a Christian to speak against his conscience. Here I stand, I can do no other; may God help me. Amen'" (*Ibid.,* p. 265).

In the face of intensifying force, intensify your faith. There is no other way. "Hold fast till I come. Behold I come quickly."

REVELATION 13:11-15, 9, 10

Then I saw another beast that rose out of the earth; it had two horns like a lamb and it spoke like a dragon. It exercises all the authority of the first beast on its behalf, and it makes the earth and its inhabitants worship the first beast, whose mortal wound had been healed.

It performs great signs, even making fire come down from heaven to earth in the sight of all, and by the signs that it is allowed to perform on behalf of the beast, it deceives the inhabitants of earth, telling them to make an image for the beast that had been wounded by the sword and yet lived; and it was allowed to give breath to the image of the beast so that the image of the beast could even speak and cause those who would not worship the image of the beast to be killed.

Let anyone who has an ear listen: If you are to be taken captive, into captivity you go; if you kill with the sword, with the sword you must be killed.

Here is a call for the endurance and faith of the saints.

3

Is the New Christian Right Wrong?

Have you ever heard of the San Francisco Bay Area Skeptics Society? I hadn't either until I read about them in the paper recently as they issued their eighth annual list of failed psychic predictions—prophecies that made tabloid headlines, but not news. Here are some of them:

❏ Maeia Graciette predicted that a massive earthquake would strike the Grand Canyon and that actor Tom Cruise would lose his hair because of a stress-related illness. But both appear to be in one piece!

❏ Judy Heavenly, another psychic, predicted that Pope John Paul II would have a "close call" with a charging "crazed camel," and that scientists would find evidence of extra-terrestrial life using the Hubble space telescope. The hard-to-focus Hubble did indeed suffer from gremlins, but only the high-tech type.

❏ Terri Brill predicted that a quake would dump California into the ocean, and that U.S. housing costs would drop by as much as 50 percent. Housing prices did slip a bit, as did the state, but Brill kept her California residency.

❏ And then an unnamed psychic predicted that Tammy Faye Bakker and Imelda Marcos would open a boutique last year. The prediction didn't state whether they would be selling shoes or Avon products. But obviously the prophecy did not come true!

So much for supermarket psychics. Pretty dumb! No, come to think of it, pretty smart! Smart, that is, if your strategy is to turn prophecies of *all* kinds into public laughingstocks! Pretty smart, if your purpose is to distract the world from the very prophecy that exposes your last *modus operandi* on a disintegrating planet. Pretty clever, come to think of it, if you're hoping against hope that this end-time civilization will not discover the truth to be found in the Apocalypse.

No. Not dumb at all. Brilliant, really, if you answer to the name Lucifer. Because if you know that your time is short, you'll try every trick in the book to keep the world from the Book. Which is precisely why in this book we're going back to the Book and some dusty apocalyptic prophecies that are disturbingly fast becoming today's troubled headlines. So come and peer behind the veil of time again, here in the second half of that haunting apocalyptic prophecy of Revelation 13.

The Second Beast

Then I saw another beast that rose out of the earth;
it had two horns like a lamb and it spoke like a
dragon. It exercises all the authority of the first
beast on its behalf, and it makes the earth and its inhabitants worship the first beast, whose mortal

> wound had been healed. It performs great signs, even
> making fire come down from heaven to earth in the
> sight of all; and by the signs that it is allowed to per-
> form on behalf of the beast, it deceives the inhabitants
> of earth, telling them to make an image for the beast
> that had been wounded by the sword and yet lived;
> and it was allowed to give breath to the image of the
> beast so that the image of the beast could even speak
> and cause those who would not worship the image of
> the beast to be killed (Revelation 13:11-15).

What's going on here? Something ominous, something terrible, something mysterious, something tragic is being predicted in this haunted piece of the Apocalypse. Who is this second beast power—this power predicted to eventually possess global dominance and control? This power that will join forces with the first beast in this very prophecy? This power that will eventually become a global policeman commanding, demanding, and finally enforcing global worship of the first beast?

Who is this second beast? What power could possibly be described here? There is only one power on earth that meets all the prophetic criteria here. Read the apocalyptic prophecy again and see for yourself.

"Then I saw another beast that rose out of the earth" (verse 11). Interestingly, the Greek verb that John chose for "that rose" is *anabaino*, which means "to grow" or "to spring up." It's the same word Matthew used in Jesus' parable of the sower to describe the growing of the thorny weed that sprang up (Matthew 13:7). So what John is describing here is a beast that springs up and comes out of nowhere, growing like a weed to assume a global role.

But please note from whence this second beast arises. Do you recall where the first beast we encountered and identified in the previous chapter came from? Read verse 1 again: "And I saw a beast rising out of *the sea*." Letting the Apocalypse interpret itself, what kind of symbolism do we encounter here? The answer is found in Revelation 17:15, where an angel describes to John the apocalyptic meaning of the symbol of water: "'The waters that you saw, where the whore is seated, are peoples and multitudes and nations and languages.'" In other words, the waters in the Apocalypse are symbolic of great masses of people and nations and languages. This means that the first beast power would arise in the midst of history's great nations and peoples. And in fact, the only geo-politico-religious power that could possibly be described as holding dominance during the Dark and Middle Ages was indeed a power that rose up in the midst of history's great peoples.

But this second power is depicted in stark contrast! For here is a beast that ascends, not out of the waters, but—by contrast—out of the earth. This rich apocalyptic symbolism diverts our attention from the water—away from the masses of history's great nations—and rivets it upon this second beast that springs to life in an unpopulated region of the world, far from history's peopled thoroughfares.

Who could this power possibly be? Ah, there is one word we left out of our examination of verse 11. And it is the first word, which the NRSV correctly and interpretatively translates, "then." But why "then"? Because there's an important sequence taking place here. Remember the first beast and how it was mortally wounded after enjoying over a millennium of global sway during the history of the Christian church? That geo-religio-political power that was brought to its knees and nearly destroyed by a mortal wound? Interestingly enough, that mortal wound is also described in the second half of chapter 13 as "the beast that had been wounded by the sword and yet lived" (verse 14).

The sword John saw was a military weapon. And that fits precisely with the historical fulfillment of the prophecy, that the first beast—the geo-religio-political power—would be mortally wounded. This fulfillment occurred in 1798 when Napoleon's military general, Berthier, took Pope Pius VI captive from Rome and shut down the papacy. A mortal wound by the sword of the military, indeed!

Note the clear sequential order depicted in these two consecutive verses. Verse 10 prophesied the first beast's captivity, which occurred in 1798: "If you are to be taken captive, into captivity you go; if you kill with the sword, with the sword you must be killed." Then immediately, in verse 11, John portrayed the next major event in this prophecy's historical pageant: "Then I saw another beast that rose out of the earth."

Who, then, is the second beast? What power on earth sprang into existence and began its comparatively rapid growth into global dominance around the 1790s? What power on earth sprang into existence far away from the waters—from the masses and multitudes, from the great nations of the Middle Ages? What power on earth sprang into existence with those credentials and today holds global sway? Given the historical background, as well as the time frame for its emergence, there is only one international power that fits the prophetic description here: late 1700s; away from Europe and the masses; growing rapidly into eventual global dominance. Only one power fits the bill. And that power is the nation of which I am a citizen—the United States of America.

With what pride I still sing the words written by that Russian immigrant, Irving Berlin, who landed on these shores back in 1893:

> *"God bless America,*
> *Land that I love;*
> *Stand beside her,*
> *And guide her,*
> *Through the night*
> *With a light from above.*
> *From the mountains,*
> *To the prairies,*
> *To the oceans white with foam,*
> *God bless America,*
> *My home sweet home."*

What American has not felt the electric thrill of emotion

while singing that prayer? Because God has blessed America in a signal way, as no other nation in modern history.

If you're a citizen of another country, I can almost hear your gracious remonstrance that I'm sounding just like an American now. Which, of course, I can't help. So listen for a moment to a foreigner—an alien in our land—and let her speak for the world.

A few weeks ago I had the privilege of joining over 1,500 men and women of the Economic Club of Southwest Michigan in attending a lecture by one of the most powerful and influential women of the world —Margaret Thatcher, former Prime Minister of the United Kingdom. I quickly grabbed my pen and scribbled down her words, when she declared that the United States "is the greatest power in the world today." She went on, "You have indeed a very, very special destiny."

A very special destiny? More than she will ever know!

Charles Krauthammer, writing in *New Republic* magazine on July 29, 1991, observed that recent events "have given birth to a highly unusual world structure with a single power, the United States, at the apex of the international system. There is no prospect in the immediate future of any power to rival the United States."

Not Japan, not Germany, not Russia.

Which is why Yassir Arafat, in responding to the sudden ascendancy of the United States in the global political arena, called Washington "The New Rome" (*Newsweek*, August 12, 1991), recalling the days of the Roman Empire's dominance. For that reason, who could be surprised at Richard Nixon's latest book, entitled *Seize the Moment: America's Challenge in a One Superpower World.* Whether you're American or not, the undisputed fact remains that the United States is at this very moment enjoying a sole global superpower status she has never in her history experienced. A status, by the way, that our leaders apparently plan never to relinquish! On March 8, 1992, the Associated Press carried the following release, datelined Washington, D.C.:

In a broad new policy statement that is in its final
drafting state, the Defense Department asserts that
America's political and military mission in the post-
Cold War era will be to ensure that no rival super-
power is allowed to emerge in Western Europe,
Asia, or the territory of the former Soviet Union.
(*South Bend Tribune.*)

In a 46-page document "that has been circulating at the
highest levels of the Pentagon for weeks," the release continues, a case is made "for a world dominated by one superpower whose position can be perpetuated by constructive
behavior and sufficient military might to deter any nation or
group of nations from challenging American primacy."

Unrivaled and unchallenged. But why? And what will
happen next?

A Sad Ending

Wouldn't it be wonderful if this apocalyptic prediction
ended with verse 11? But tragically, the prophecy hurries on
to an ending both sobering and utterly sad. It ends like a
Shakespearean tragedy for this nation that I love.

Yes, there was a divine destiny in our birth. Yes, I do
believe to the very depths of my being that God did indeed
raise up this nation over 200 years ago, right on schedule with
this apocalyptic prophecy. After all, it was to be a new,
radically bold experiment "with liberty and justice for all."
An experiment begun by a scant shipload of men, women,
and children who fled to these shores in search of freedom.

And what did they long for? What were they looking for?
As one writer so aptly put it, they came in search of "a country
without a king and a church without a pope." The twin legacies
of liberty: civil liberty and religious liberty. We have declared
them to be our unalienable and God-given right. No other
nation in the history of this planet has so powerfully championed
those twin legacies of the human race—civil and religious

freedom—leading some commentators to conclude that the two horns of this lamb-like beast are indeed those twin legacies of civil freedom and religious liberty.

The words of Emma Lazarus inscribed on the Statue of Liberty in New York's harbor have rung true in the breasts of this planet's exiles:

> *Give me your tired, your poor, your huddled masses*
> *yearning to breathe free, the wretched refuse of your*
> *teeming shore. Send these, the homeless, tempest-tossed*
> *to me. I lift my lamp beside the golden door!*

Land of the free and home of the brave. But something tragic goes wrong! At the very time she achieves global dominance and influence, look what happens to her: "Then I saw another beast that rose out of the earth; it had two horns like a lamb and it spoke like a dragon. It exercises all the authority of the first beast on its behalf, and it makes the earth and its inhabitants worship the first beast, whose mortal wound had been healed" (verses 11, 12).

Please note that it is after the healing of the wound that the United States will achieve her global dominance and sway. And so far, history is right on schedule!

But what seems so unbelievable is the startlingly plain revelation of Verse 12. This second beast power will command not only her own citizens, but the population of the entire planet, to worship and follow the first beast of this apocalyptic chapter.

Sounds simply impossible, given the guarantees provided by the Constitution of the United States and the Bill of Rights? Impossible that this nation could turn out as the Apocalypse predicts?

It does seem utterly impossible, doesn't it—at first glance and on first thought? For I, too, have read the Bill of Rights. In fact, I have a facsimile copy of it hanging on the wall behind my study desk. The Bill of Rights is the first ten amendments to what Gladstone, one of the greatest English prime ministers of all time, referred to as "The most wonderful work ever struck off at a given time by the brain and purpose of man"—the Constitution of the United States of America. During her speech, I heard Margaret Thatcher call it "the most marvelous Constitution."

Read again the First Amendment: "Congress shall make no law respecting an establishment of religion, or prohibiting the free exercise thereof; or abridging the freedom of speech, or of the press; or the right of the people peaceably to assemble, and to petition the government for the redress of grievances."

By the way, did you know that religion is only mentioned twice in the entire document, including the Bill of Rights: once in Article 6, where it states that religion is not to be used as a test for public office, and then here in the First Amendment. Which leads Clifford Goldstein, in his book *The Saving of America*, to conclude:

> The only time religion is mentioned in the Constitution is to stop the government from making laws that would either establish, discriminate against, or prohibit it. If the government is not allowed to make laws regarding religion, then it will never be able to persecute or discriminate against on the basis of religion. Here is the secret of America's great religious freedoms! (Pacific Press Publishing Assoc., Boise, Idaho, 1988, p. 37)

Jefferson called it the wall of separation between church and state—between government and religion. So how could the day ever come when this mighty, freedom-loving nation would ever abrogate or abandon this first amendment? The government of the United States enforcing religious observance upon its citizens? Impossible!

The New Christian Right

Yes, impossible. Until, that is, you meet the New Christian Right—a group of sincere, but sincerely wrong Americans who have begun to tamper with the Bill of Rights. Who are they? Listen again to Penny Lernoux, Roman Catholic journalist, in her book *People of God: The Struggle for World Catholicism:*

> In the United States fundamentalism is often associ-
> ated with the movement of born-again Christians
> who believe in the inerrancy of the Bible and the doc-
> trine of creationism. . . . Regardless of theological dif-
> ferences, religious fundamentalists share certain
> characteristics, such as a reverence for authority and
> fear of secularization—or "secular humanism," as the
> Vatican and U.S. evangelicals call it. They also insist
> that they alone possess the truth, and they usually
> align themselves with the political right. In the United
> States they have been called the New Right to distin-
> guish them from the traditional forms of political and
> religious conservatism. Among the New Right's activ-
> ists are fundamentalist Catholics who yearn for an
> "old-time religion," found today chiefly in the Polish
> pope's homeland, and who have made common
> cause with Reagan's evangelical supporters. (Penguin
> Books, New York, 1989, pp. 10, 11).

Anybody who reads and watches the news today knows that there is a new religio-political coalition uniting Protestant, Catholic, and Jewish Americans in a renewed attempt to spiritually reform America. Their rallying point initially began with a common cause: an anti-abortion battle in this nation. Which is why Cardinal O'Connor of New York and James Dobson of Focus on the Family—who has done so much for the American family—can join hands in a concerted effort to outlaw abortion. I, too, am opposed to the wholesale slaughter of human fetuses as a method of birth control. But I find it more than strangely coincidental that in this particular hour of history, there is such an apparently innocuous joining of some very strange bedfellows, as they clasp hands together in a new common cause. And if they work so well in this cause, I wonder what new cause they might eventually find on which to effectively unite.

How serious are they? Listen now to Frederick Clarkson,

an investigative journalist based in Washington D.C., who frequently writes about the Religious Right, as he did in the January 14, 1992, issue of *Church and State* magazine:

> When I slipped into the national leadership meeting of Pat Robertson's [lawyer/minister and speaker/director of the Christian Broadcasting Network and the nationally popular 700 Club] Christian Coalition, I thought I knew what to expect. . . . But I was unprepared for what I saw, heard and felt . . . for two days in November during the "Road to Victory" Conference and Strategy Briefing. . . . I was . . . surprised to see a rapidly growing, technologically sophisticated religio-political organization, built largely from Robertson's 1988 presidential campaign (p. 4).

Who are the members of this Christian Coalition? Read on:

> The Christian Coalition claims it is an "issues-oriented" organization of "Evangelicals, pro-family Catholics and their allies" working to "reverse the moral decline in America and reaffirm our godly heritage." . . . Former Reagan White House Domestic Policy chief (and now head of James Dobson's Family Research Council [which is a political action group in Washington, D.C., whose newsletter is published by Focus on the Family]) Gary Bauer said, "Obviously this conference is about the 1992 elections. . . . We are engaged in a social, political and cultural civil war" (p. 6).

Two powers uniting to make war. Does this sound familiar? Of the first power, the Apocalypse declares, "It was allowed to make war on the saints and to conquer them" (verse 7). Of the second power, we read, "It exercises all the authority of the first beast on its behalf, and it makes the earth and its inhabitants worship the first beast, whose mortal wound had been healed" (verse 12).

Mark it carefully: We are no longer dealing with some sort of backwater, two-bit, redneck fundamentalism in the New Christian Right. By their own admission, they are out for war! Which is exactly how James Dobson put it in his January, 1992, *Focus on the Family* newsletter: "The trends I've reported in this letter should confirm for us . . . that the majority of Americans believe in the Judeo-Christian system of values. [But] the civil war is far from over, and the eventual outcome still hangs in the balance."

As Bauer aptly put it, these are people who are out for war—a religious civil war. Listen to how Pat Robertson was introduced at a recent conference by a Louisiana pastor, Billy McCormack, who declared "that in the two centuries since Washington and Jefferson, 'the forces of evil have coalesced. They've formed a mighty tide of approaching destruction.' Providentially, God has raised up (another) man from Virginia to lead America in the rediscovery of its soul" (p. 6).

May I be candid with you? I am afraid for the soul of this nation should that man and his coalition ever get to the place where he and they wield any greater power over the interpretation of the Bill of Rights. For he and his colleagues are on public record decrying the wall of separation between church and state in this country. Pat Robertson claims that the phrase, "separation of church and state," can be linked to the Russian Constitution, but not ours. His cohort, W. A. Criswell, a leading Baptist minister and the final speaker at the 1984 Republican Convention in Dallas, declared: "I believe that this notion of the separation of church and state was the figment of some infidel's imagination" (Goldstein, p. 59).

It no longer takes any imagination to figure out what in fact is going on out there! The New Christian Right is wrong in their interpretation of church-state separation. But they've got one thing right: We are truly in a war! "The dragon was angry with the woman, and went off to make war on the rest of her children" (Revelation 12:17). The twin legacies of civil and religious freedom are under attack, incredibly, by Christians in our nation today. The

Apocalypse foretells the tragic eventual outcome for this liberty-loving land.

Even the United States Supreme Court—one of the greatest judicial bodies that sits anywhere on this planet—has ominously changed its historic defense of the wall of separation between government and religion. Supreme Court Justice Wiley Rutledge could write in 1947, "We have staked the very existence of our country on the faith that complete separation between state and religion is best for the state and best for religion." In stark contrast, our present Supreme Court Chief Justice, William Rehnquist, declares, "The 'wall of separation between church and state' is a metaphor based on bad history, a metaphor which has proved useless as a guide to judging. It should be frankly and explicitly abandoned" (Goldstein, pp. 59, 60).

Rehnquist is not alone. One by one, under strong lobbying pressure from the New Christian Right, Ronald Reagan and George Bush have nominated jurists to the bench who have tilted the balance of the Court to a new conservatism that is challenging the historic and constitutional protection of the wall separating church and state in this nation.

> Then I saw another beast that rose out of the earth;
> it had two horns like a lamb and it spoke like a
> dragon. It exercises all the authority of the first
> beast on its behalf, and it makes the earth and its in-
> habitants worship the first beast, whose mortal
> wound had been healed (Revelation 13:11, 12).

The Dragon's strategy is always innocuous in the beginning. Lucifer's *modus operandi* has ever been a quiet stealing of the march upon the unsuspecting. So when the December 9, 1991, issue of *Time* magazine came out with a new cover story, its international readership certainly expected a fair and balanced treatment of the subject. After all, *Time* is a world-class news journal that has earned its prestigious reputation for accurate and penetrating journalism.

But was it this time? Cover story: "One Nation, Under God." Subtitle: "Has the Separation of Church and State Gone Too Far?" It was, of course, only a rhetorical question. But obviously, the editors believe that the answer is Yes.

> In this nation of spiritual paradoxes, it is legal to hang a picture in a public exhibit of a crucifix submerged in urine, or to utter virtually any conceivable blasphemy in a public place; it is not legal, the federal courts have ruled, to mention God reverently in a classroom, on a football field or at a commencement ceremony as part of a public prayer (p. 62).

Through a strategic juxtaposition of selected judicial rulings, the editors have stacked the emotional deck against their readers. Clifford Goldstein is absolutely right:

> What is displayed in a public museum where people can choose to go or to avoid, and what happens in a classroom where children are forced by law to attend, are two different things. Plus, who can't mention God reverently on a football field? Today half the NFL is out there on their knees begging the Almighty to give them the power to bash their opponents to pieces (*Liberty Alert*, February/ March, 1992).

The New Christian Right's radically conservative sway is permeating even our national press. Look at how *Time* framed one of its questions in its poll on the subject of the separation of church and state: "Do you favor or oppose allowing children to say prayers in public schools?"

Talk about a loaded question! As Goldstein exclaimed:

> They might have well asked, "Do you favor or oppose homosexual, HIV-positive, drug-addicted child pornographers teaching in public schools?" The issue in church-state separation has nothing to do with being allowed to pray. No one is going to send a kid to the principal's office for praying

privately. This isn't the former Communist Alba-
nia. The real issue involves government *sponsorship
and endorsement* of prayer in public schools. Somehow, those who framed that question left the part
about government sponsorship—the real issue—
out. How convenient (*Ibid.*).

Listen, if we give the government the right to tell us when
to pray, what will stop them from telling us when to worship?
Nothing! "And it makes the earth and its inhabitants worship
the first beast, whose mortal wound had been healed" (verse
12). In the end, the very end, nothing will stop them!

Which is why the New Christian Right is wrong. The
tragic lessons of the Dark and Middle Ages still have not been
learned. For when church and state, religion and politics, join
hands together, the crimson tread of oppression is only a
footstep away. The millions of martyrs during that dark
millennium are proof enough!

Overnight

Some may wonder, How can this new movement possibly
be wrong with so many powerful and popular Christian
leaders clamoring for government support of religious convictions? Jerry Falwell, James Kennedy, Tim LaHaye, Pat
Robertson, Robert Schuller, Oral Roberts, James Dobson,
Pope John Paul II. But then, what did you think the dragon
was going to do? Start off with a death decree for all who
refuse to obey the command to worship the first beast? Are
you kidding? Everybody knows that the best way to tear
down a wall (if your intent is clandestine and secretive) is to
do it one brick at a time. Because then maybe nobody will
notice; maybe nobody will speak up.

Mark it carefully: The wall *is* coming down, one brick at a
time. And liberty-loving Americans, Christian or otherwise,
must lift their voices in warning opposition to this dangerous
course! Because when that wall comes down, everybody will
lose. The entire nation will be lost. Mark those words.

Is the day coming? Is it nearer than when we first believed? I tremble for my country; I tremble for my church. Are we ready? Are we watching? Is anybody awake?

Eight decades ago, this single-line prediction was written: ". . . the final movements will be rapid ones" (*Testimonies for the Church*, Vol. 9, p. 11). Only within the last few months have we learned how dramatically true those words could be as we have witnessed the lightning speed with which global change can shatter history's headlines forever. *Overnight.*

The Berlin Wall. The Kremlin coup. Good-bye Gorbachev, hello Boris. A free Europe. A new geo-religio-political leader for the world. One superpower left. How did that Department of Defense policy statement that we noted earlier in this chapter put it? "A world dominated by one superpower whose position can be perpetuated . . . to deter any nation or group of nations from challenging American primacy." Overnight. All of it overnight.

A few weeks ago I received the following press release, faxed to me from Sweden and translated by a friend there. It was carried in the Swedish Lutheran State Church *Newsletter*, August 15, 1991:

> In October [1991], for the first time ever, an ecumenical worship service at St. Peter's Cathedral in Rome will take place. Heads of state from Sweden, Finland, and Poland are invited together with clerical representatives in order to celebrate the 600-years anniversary of the canonization of St. Bridget. [She was from Sweden, spent her later life in Rome and her relics are enshrined in a Lutheran church in Sweden. Her daughter, also canonized, is buried in St. Peter's Cathedral.]
>
> Behind this ecumenical worship service is a strong engagement on the part of the Pope, says Heinz-Albert Raem, responsible for Lutheran matters at Rome's Pontifical Council for the Promotion of Christian Unity. According to Raem, the ongoing

dialogue with the Lutherans is one of the most important for the Catholic Church: "The Lutherans have clearly expressed that they want to achieve Christian unity. Certainly, such clearly stated goals cannot be found in all dialogues. Therefore, this dialogue is very important to the Vatican."

Now note carefully the time frame in which this spokesman for the Vatican's Council for the Promotion of Christian Unity is operating. His words are startling:

> On the question regarding the goal of this dialogue and its future, Heinz-Albert Raem, who is German, . . . continues: "It is the same question as when people surmised about the fall of the Berlin Wall. Some people said it would never happen. But I am convinced that the wall that certainly exists between us Catholics and the Lutherans, but which is broken through in many places, will tumble down. *But this will happen suddenly and unexpectedly, exactly as did the Berlin Wall on November 9, 1989*" (italics supplied).

A Vatican spokesman without equivocation declares that the wall of separation between Rome and Lutherans will come down as "suddenly and unexpectedly" as did the Berlin Wall!

The wall is coming down. The Apocalypse is coming true with pulse-quickening precision. "The final movements will be rapid ones." Overnight. Like the Berlin Wall. Overnight. Is that possible with the Bill of Rights? Can that wall come down, too? It already is, brick by brick. But one day you and I will awaken to the horrible discovery that—overnight—the wall has at last come down. (If Congress can vote itself a pay raise at 1 a.m. in order to avoid the public outcry and clamor, what else could our heavily lobbied legislators be induced to enact overnight?)

It is time to wake up, America. It is time to wake up, fellow Christians. Listen to the Apocalypse!

REVELATION 13:11, 12, 15; 15:2-4

Then I saw another beast that rose out of the earth; it had two horns like a lamb and it spoke like a dragon. It exercises all the authority of the first beast on its behalf, and it makes the earth and its inhabitants worship the first beast, whose mortal wound had been healed.

And it was allowed to give breath to the image of the beast so that the image of the beast could even speak and cause those who would not worship the image of the beast to be killed.

And I saw what appeared to be a sea of glass mixed with fire, and those who had conquered the beast and its image and the number of its name, standing beside the sea of glass with harps of God in their hands.

And they sing the song of Moses, the servant of God, and the song of the Lamb: "Great and amazing are your deeds, Lord God Almighty! Just and true are your ways, King of the nations!

"Lord, who will not fear and glorify your name? For you alone are holy.

"All nations will come and worship before you, for your judgments have been revealed."

4

A Loyalty That Could Get You Killed

Minorities in America

Well-known Pulitzer Prize winning historian and biographer Arthur Schlesinger, presently Albert Schweitzer Professor of Humanities at the City University of New York, has sounded an ominous modern-day prediction with a familiar apocalyptic ring.

In a December 11, 1991 *Wall Street Journal* essay, he sought to define the global unrest that has descended upon a post-communist civilization. His title: "A New Era Begins—But History Remains."

And then appears this boxed highlight: "As the warfare of ideologies subsides, the world re-enters a possibly more dangerous era of ethnic and racial warfare. Yugoslavia's tragedy is only the most murderous portent."

Near the end of his essay is an observation that ought to be a flashing red light for those who are finding in the Apocalypse today a very present history. Note his words carefully:

> What makes the current situation worse today is that the world faces a spreading recession that will intensify every grievance, every antagonism, every hatred. As good times ease entry into full membership in a national community, so hard times sharpen animosity and conflict. Unemployment, especially among the young, poisons human and social relations. People who can't find jobs look around for some other to blame—the blacks or the Jews or the immigrants. If the U.S. goes into depression, it will not be a melting pot. It will be a boiling pot.

Did you catch it? This eminent historian predicts that the intensification of economic hardship will lead this nation to sharpen its animosities and look for some minority to blame. When times get tough, the tough go looking for somebody else to blame. It's an American ritual. Which is why Japan-bashing is so popular these days. (And I don't say that just because I was "Made in Japan," having been born and having lived the first fourteen years of my life in the Land of the Rising Sun.) But isn't it intriguing that this historian would observe that when times get bad, the minorities get blamed. It recalls to mind a line I once read in that apocalyptic classic *The Great Controversy:*

> Those who honor God [will be] accused of bringing judgments upon the world, and they will be regarded as the cause of the fearful convulsions of nature and the strife and bloodshed among men that are filling the earth with woe (p. 614).

Schlesinger says that historically, Americans are inclined to blame their economic woes on some minority. And the Apocalypse says that in the end, Schlesinger will be right.

Minorities in the Apocalypse

And I saw a beast rising out of the sea, having ten
horns and seven heads; and on its horns were ten
diadems, and on its heads were blasphemous
names. . . . One of its heads seemed to have received a death-blow, but its mortal wound had
been healed. In amazement the whole earth followed the beast. . . . Then I saw another beast that
rose out of the earth; it had two horns like a lamb
and it spoke like a dragon. It exercises all the
authority of the first beast on its behalf, and it
makes the earth and its inhabitants worship the
first beast, whose mortal wound had been healed
(Revelation 13:1, 3, 11, 12).

Here they are again—the two apocalyptic beast powers
who, according to the prophetic Word, will unite in a final
confederacy against God. And who are these two historical,
global powers? In the previous two chapters, we carefully
documented the internal evidence and descriptions within
this prophecy that identify these two powers with historical
accuracy.

The first beast is the geo-religio-political power that dominated the Dark and Middle Ages history of the Christian
Church. Wounded at the end of its over 1,200-year dominance
by a military blow, this power was nearly destroyed. But the
ancient prophecy predicted that the mortal wound would
eventually heal. Subsequently, this power would achieve phenomenal global ascendancy and dominance. A dominance that
is building today with breathtaking rapidity.

We have noted (and the disclaimer is worth repeating)
that this power is precisely that—a *power*, and not any next-
door neighbor; it is an institution, not an on-the-job individual; it is a system, not someone you happen to know. But
regarding this institution, we have carefully noted that there
is only one power in the history of Christendom that matches

this apocalyptic description. And that power is the institution of the Roman papacy.

The second beast power springs into existence far from Europe and the masses of humanity right at the time the first beast power is wounded in the 1790s—a power that would eventually become a world leader with enough global dominance to command the entire world to follow it. In the previous chapter we have noted that the United States of America is in fact the sole power that matches the global, historical parameters of this prophecy.

President George Bush, in his State of the Union address in January, 1992 looked back on the upheaval of 1991 as being fraught with changes of "almost biblical proportions." He went on to declare that "by the grace of God America won the Cold War," so that the United States today is the "one sole and preeminent power" on earth.

Amazingly, this prophecy predicted that both powers would achieve their global dominance at the same time! The healing of the wound of the first power would coincide with the rise to global leadership of the second power. So that in the end, they join together in a final confederacy.

Enter the United States government's appointment, at the insistence of President Ronald Reagan, of a U.S. ambassador to the Vatican—an action that broke ranks with our historical precedent of the separation of church and state. It not only defies the intent and protection of the First Amendment of the Constitution—it violates it. Since when does the government—ours or any other government for that matter—appoint an ambassador to a church? Ambassadors belong to political and sovereign nations. (Which ought to be an apocalyptic clue in and of itself!)

The illogical nature of this governmental action was exposed when W. Kenneth Dam of the State Department was asked in a U.S. House of Representatives hearing why we should have an Ambassador to the Holy See. His reply: "It would allow the United States to influence the political positions of the Roman Catholic Church" (James Dunn,

Perpectives in Religion, p. 152). And therein lies the violation—government becoming entangled in religion, and all in the name of politics. And how many churches does the U.S. have an ambassador to serve? Only one—Rome.

"Let anyone who has an ear listen" (Revelation 13:9).

While in Washington, D.C., a few weeks ago, I visited with a church official who had recently returned from a trip through Latin America. He asked that I not mention the name of the country, but one government there is now debating a bill that would require religious teachers of all denominations to be certified by the government and by the Roman Catholic Church. Furthermore, this law would provide a free tract of land for the Roman Catholic Church in all future housing developments in that nation. All other churches wishing to build in those same developments would be required to apply to the government for permission. Talk about the entanglement of church and state—it is daily fare in Latin America!

But will it become a daily reality in North America?

> It [the second beast power] performs great signs,
> even making fire come down from heaven to earth
> in the sight of all; and by the signs that it is allowed
> to perform on behalf of the beast [first beast
> power], it deceives the inhabitants of earth, telling
> them to make an image for the beast that had been
> wounded by the sword and yet lived; and it was al-
> lowed to give breath to the image of the beast so
> that the image of the beast could even speak and
> cause those who would not worship the image of
> the beast to be killed (Revelation 13:13-15).

"An image to the beast"—what could that possibly be? The second power—the United States—creates an image to the first power—Rome. But what does this mean, and how could it come about? First, please note that the Greek word for image is *eikon*, from whence we get our word *icon*. Images . . . icons . . . what are they? Are they not simply replicas, likenesses, imitations resembling the real thing? So when the second power makes an image to the first beast power, we would expect that image to look very much like the first beast, would we not? A replica.

But what would a replica of the first beast power be? Would it not be a system patterned after the geo-religio-political power that dominated the Dark Ages, during which some historians estimate that untold millions of men, women, and children were martyred for their faith? Would not the apocalyptic "image" to that Middle Ages power mean a replication or an imitation of her *modus operandi* at the end of time? Would not the apocalyptic "image to the beast" represent a religio-political entanglement and confederacy that will legislate a religious observance of the church and be enforced by the state? According to the Apocalypse, what happened for over a millennium in the Middle Ages and has been happening for centuries in Latin America will one day happen in this nation and the world, at the high price of human lives:

> And it was allowed to give breath to the image of the beast . . . and cause those who would not worship the image of the beast to be killed. Also it causes all, both small and great, both rich and poor, both free and slave, to be marked on the right hand or the forehead, so that no one can buy or sell who does not have the mark, that is, the name of the beast or the number of its name. This calls for wisdom: let anyone with understanding calculate the number of the beast, for it is the number of a person. Its number is six hundred sixty-six (Revelation 13:15-18).

A Question of Loyalty

And what will be the issue that galvanizes this final entanglement—this last showdown? Note it carefully: The final question to be settled on earth will be the question of loyalty. To which authority will you be loyal? There is no question that biblically, the final conflict is depicted here in the Apocalypse in the context of loyalty to an authority. And the searing question all the way through the prophecy is: Whose authority will you choose—to whom will you be loyal?

And in the the end you will have only two choices. Will you choose the religio-political authority of the two beasts' confederacy, which will threaten with extermination all those who refuse to worship at their temple? Or will you choose the authority of the Creator God, who urgently dispatches an end-time appeal to His dying creation through His Three Angels: "Fear God and give him glory, for the hour of his judgment has come; and worship him who made heaven and earth, the sea and the springs of water" (Revelation 14:7).

Indeed, the last question to be decided in human history is one of loyalty and allegiance: Whom will you worship, the Creator God of the universe—or the beastly creation of a substitute image? In the end, the entire planet will make the choice.

It has been a choice we have faced from the very beginning. For, like a golden thread, the divine gift of the seventh-day Sabbath is woven throughout the Scriptures—from the creation story in Genesis to the new earth story in Revelation. Before sin came along, the seventh-day Sabbath existed (Genesis 2:1-3). Before the Ten Commandments were given, God's people observed the seventh-day Sabbath (Exodus 16:4, 22-30). The seventh-day Sabbath was embedded in the heart of the Decalogue (Exodus 20:8-11). When God became one with us, Jesus consistently observed the seventh-day Sabbath (Luke 4:16). He revealed Himself as the very Lord of the Sabbath (Matthew 12:8)—the One who instituted the Sabbath as God and observed it as Man. After He ascended, His disciples continued to worship on the seventh-day Sabbath (Acts 13:14-16, 42, 44; 16:12, 13; 17:2; 18:1-4). And the redeemed of all ages—the victors of the Apocalypse—will worship the Creator throughout eternity on the seventh-day Sabbath (Isaiah 66:22, 23).

But why God's insistence on the seventh day? Because from the very beginning, He insituted it to be a perpetual *sign* that He is the Lord who created us (Exodus 20:8-11; 31:17; Ezekiel 20:20). Which means that at the very heart of the Sabbath, we encounter a God who longs to be in personal relationship with us. For that reason, when the human race fell victim to the dragon's deception, God further vested the Sabbath as a sign that He is the One—the only One—who can save us (Exodus 31:13; Ezekiel 20:12; Hebrews 4:4-11). The Sabbath is a day to remember Him—from a God who remembered us.

But it's a day we've forgotten. Which is why God's fourth commandment begins with the word *Remember.* "Remember the sabbath day, and keep it holy" (Exodus 20:8). Not one day in seven, but the seventh one (Exodus 20:11)—a day locked forever in the human weekly cycle. A perpetual reminder that our Creator is the only God who can save us.

No wonder Lucifer is so deathly intent on obliterating the Sabbath. For if he can blot out that divine-human memorial to creation, then the world can be ripped wide open to accept the rebel's counter-authority to God. Ripped open, indeed! His diabolical strategy has with frightening precision carved the divine image out of humanity's heart. Charles Darwin and Karl Marx bequeathed to civilization two Creator-less theories that have neutered the human race and left us godless orphans on the abandoned streets of time.

The dragon is nobody's fool. Lucifer's scheme worked. With evolutionism and communism eroding the intellectual and political fronts over the past century, all the dragon has needed is a bridge into the heart of Christendom—the one realm still devoted to the Creator. In the healing of the first beast power within this century, the dragon has found that bridge at last. That means "he's got the whole world in his hands"—almost. Just like God, who he's always wanted to be.

"In amazement the whole earth followed the beast. They worshiped the dragon, for he had given his authority to the beast" (Revelation 13:3, 4). "How you are fallen from heaven, O Day Star, son of Dawn! . . . You said in your heart, 'I will ascend to heaven; I will raise my throne above the stars of God; . . . I will make myself like the Most High'" (Isaiah 14:12-14).

How art thou fallen, O Lucifer, Dragon of the Apocalypse.

You see, in the end we are again reminded: It will be Lucifer against the Lamb, Satan against Christ, the rebel against God—the God Incarnate, who, when He was here among us for a while, declared, "The Son of Man is Lord of the Sabbath" (Matthew 12:8). And the Lord of the Sabbath became the Lord of the cross. Do you know why? Because the church and the state united to destroy this same Jesus who would not bow to their combined religio-political authority. So they killed Him. And when they did, the Lord of the Sabbath became the Lord of the cross.

Two thousand years ago, church and state united to destroy the Lord of the Sabbath. Two thousand years later, church and state will unite to destroy the Sabbath of the Lord. Lucifer hasn't changed. If he can't destroy the Lord of the Sabbath, then he will seek to destroy the Sabbath of the Lord.

For that reason, God brackets the apocalyptic showdown depicted in Revelation 13 with identical statements that identify His last-day followers with an intensified faith and an uncompromising obedience to His commandments. As a prologue to chapter 13, Revelation 12:17 declares that God's end-time children "keep the commandments of God and hold the testimony of Jesus." And as an epilogue to the thirteenth chapter, Revelation 14:12 identifies "the saints" as "those who keep the commandments of God and hold to the faith of Jesus." It is as if God did not want to depict the final showdown without clearly identifying His final people. And what kind of people are they? A people who hold fast to Jesus with an intensified faith that manifests itself in obedience to the commandments of God.

Moreover, according to some eminent textual scholars, the fourth commandment—"Remember the sabbath day, and keep it holy . . . For in six days the Lord made heaven and earth, the sea, and all that is in them, but rested the seventh day; therefore the Lord blessed the sabbath day and consecrated it" (Exodus 20:8-11)—is alluded to directly in God's final appeal for a heavenward alignment of loyalties:

"Worship him who made heaven and earth, the sea and the springs of water" (Revelation 14:7). Thus, through this cryptic clue, the Sabbath emerges in Revelation as the ultimate test of loyalties when the apocalyptic showdown reaches its peak.

If you were Lucifer, and you craved the worship of this fallen planet, what logical posture would you assume toward the Sabbath? Since the seventh-day Sabbath is a sign and symbol of God's sole prerogative to receive our worship as our Creator and Redemmer (see Revelation 4:11), what would you set out to do? Lucifer's *modus operandi* has always been to deceive, through his own creation (he's always wanted to be a creator) of a counterfeit—not quite the real thing, but close enough that people are deceived by it and tricked into turning from God to himself. Since he has a counterfeit for everything else of God's, wouldn't it be unlike him *not* to create a counterfeit for God's sign of authority in the seventh-day Sabbath?

No one should be surprised, then, when the power represented by the first beast goes on public record in the way that it has in *The Convert's Catechism of Catholic Doctrine* (B. Herder Book Company, St. Louis, Missouri, 1942). The imprimaturs that line the introductory pages of this book are sufficient evidence that the priest-author, Peter Geiermann, was given all the ecclesiastical blessing necessary for this book to speak for Rome. Note this very enlightening series of questions and answers:

Q. Which is the Sabbath day?
A. Saturday is the Sabbath day.
Q. Why do we observe Sunday instead of Saturday?
A. We observe Sunday instead of Saturday because the Catholic Church, in the Council of Laodicea (A.D. 336), transferred the solemnity from Saturday to Sunday.
Q. Why did the Catholic Church substitute Sunday for Saturday?
A. The Church substituted Sunday for Saturday, because Christ rose from the dead on a Sunday,

and the Holy Ghost descended upon the Apostles
on a Sunday.
Q. By what authority did the Church substitute
Sunday for Saturday?
A. The Church substituted Sunday for Saturday by
the plenitude of that divine power which Jesus
Christ bestowed upon her (p. 50).

"In amazement the whole earth followed the beast" (Revelation 13:3).

Even if for only economic convenience! The October 11-17, 1991, issue of the *European* carried this eye-catching headline: "Battle lines drawn over Europe-wide day of rest." In an article by Nigel Dudley and Ian Mather, the report stated that "millions of Europeans could lose the right to work on Sundays and thousands more face the sack if EC [European Community, the new economic federation of Europe] bureaucrats succeed in making the seventh day one of compulsory rest." *

But there's more. "Countries with widely different social and working customs would have to conform to strict rules if the Sunday proposals become law. All but essential services would be banned. Even lorries [trucks] could be stopped from using motorways." Apparently the new plan "has been pushed through the European Commission with the minimum of publicity." But the plan is gathering support from Germany, the Netherlands, Luxembourg, and Denmark, "whose strict labour laws prevent virtually any trade being done on the seventh day."

What is troubling is that this new European plan has all the earmarks of the economic ban described by the Apocalypse (Revelation 13:16, 17)! And in Germany the plan already works! There "the ban on Sunday trading is

---

*So all of Europe is going to worship on the seventh-day Sabbath? No, the article speaks of the seventh-day *Sunday*. In an interesting twist, business calendars in the United States, as well as in Europe and Asia, now portray Monday as the first day of the week. (And in business terms, it usually is. Of course, the change was made strictly for convenience. But one wonders whose convenience was served in the end.) Hence, the article refers to Sunday as the seventh day.

constitutionally enshrined and 82 per cent of workers do not work on Sundays." A German politician, Elmar Brok, is quoted as saying that "Sunday was the best day for the family to have free time together." And who would want to fight the family?

How did the catechism put it? "We observe Sunday instead of Saturday because the Catholic Church... transferred the solemnity from Saturday to Sunday."

And how did the Apocalypse put it?

> [The second beast power] exercises all the authority of the first beast on its behalf, and it makes the earth and its inhabitants worship the first beast, whose mortal wound had been healed. . . . It deceives the inhabitants of earth, telling them to make an image for the beast . . . and it was allowed to give breath to the image of the beast . . . and cause those who would not worship the image of the beast to be killed (Revelation 13:12, 13, 15).

The dragon is nobody's fool. Whether the reasons are economic, social, religious, or simply convenient, the dragon doesn't care. Whether the battleground is in Europe, the United States, Latin America, Asia, or Africa, his ultimate and ulterior strategy remains the same: counterfeit the Creator and countermand His Sabbath. To finally receive the adulation and adoration of the world has always been Lucifer's driving quest. And the tragic prophetic prediction is that the world *en masse* will fulfill that lifelong dream. Lucifer doesn't care two bits about the two beasts. Their confederacy is simply a front for his own insatiable hunger for self-worship. And in the end, he'll get it! "In amazement the whole earth . . . worshiped the dragon" (Revelation 13:3, 4).

He will get the whole world, except for a handful like Shadrach, Meshach, and Abednego, who were also forced to choose between their loyalty to God and the worship of an image, Nebuchadnezzar's golden image—the monstrous creation of church and state united to enforce public worship.

With the veins bulging from his livid neck, the king raged at those three Hebrew followers of God, "And I'm going to kill you, do you hear me? I'm going to destroy the three of you if you don't bow down and worship my image. I'll give you one more chance, and then it's the furnace!"

God's loyal minority of three gazed back into the enraged royal countenance. "O king, live forever, but even if it means death, we will not bow down and worship this image." (See Daniel 3.)

Why? *Because the only loyalty worth living for is the loyalty that's worth dying for.* But if Shadrach, Meshach, and Abednego don't arrest your attention; if the Apocalypse doesn't awaken your soul; then maybe you'll listen to Robert Wong, a Seventh-day Adventist pastor from the communist People's Republic of China. He is a doctoral student at Andrews University, and recently I interviewed him before the congregation of the Pioneer Memorial Church here on our campus. Listen to a tale of loyalty.

A Loyalty Worth Dying For

Dwight K. Nelson: While you now reside in Hong Kong, it hasn't always been your home. Share with us the beginning of your story.

ROBERT WONG: I was born in Shanghai, China. My parents were both Buddhists, and my family faithfully followed the ancient traditions of that religion.

DKN: Were you communists?

WONG: No. My childhood days were before the establishment of communism in China. My father was a businessman, and our home was Buddhist.

DKN: But somewhere along the way you were introduced to the Seventh-day Adventist Church. How could that possibly have happened?

WONG: It was actually through my older brother. One day while walking down one of the streets in Shanghai, he noticed a poster advertising some meetings by an American speaker, Fordyce Detamore. My brother was studying in a Catholic high school. And because most of his textbooks were written in English, he looked at that poster and decided that they could surely improve his English. So he attended a meeting. He went to learn more English, but in that very first meeting the Holy Spirit caught his heart!

DKN: And so your older brother, who wanted to master English, ended up meeting the Master of the earth instead. Incredible! And so, Bob, he made the decision that he would follow Jesus, not only the Lord of salvation, but also the Lord of the Sabbath. So what happened to you—the kid brother who was watching him?

WONG: Well, I could tell that something profound had come over my brother. And the more I watched him, the more impressed I became with whatever it was that he had discovered. I got hold of a Bible and began to study it on my own. And it was then that I made the same discovery and met the same Jesus he had met. I gave my life to God and dedicated myself to serving Him, and I became a Seventh-day Adventist Christian.

DKN: But your story is really only beginning. Along the way you sensed the call of Christ to pastoral ministry. Where did you go to seminary?

WONG: During those early days I was working in our Seventh-day Adventist church in Shanghai. But the state church in China, known as the Three Self Church, had a requirement that for anybody to pastor in China, it was required that such an individual attend the Three Self Church seminary.

DKN: So there was a state church for a time in China? All Protestant and Catholic churches united?

WONG: No, the Three Self Church was actually a union of all Protestant churches. The Catholic Church was not a part of it.

DKN: So you attended seminary in order to continue your pastoring. Then along came 1958. What happened?

WONG: During 1958 all the churches in China were forced by the government to unite even further. Not by the Holy Spirit; not by coming to the same Truth; it was simply a government action forced upon the churches. And as a consequence, 90 percent of the churches were closed down, and the pastors were forced to find other work. But before they could reenter the workforce in our country, these pastors were required to attend a political study class.

DKN: Did you attend?

WONG: Because the classes were conducted on Saturday, I did not. And I was eventually expelled from the class.

DKN: Expelled for your convictions regarding the Sabbath?

WONG: That's correct. But before they expelled me, they called a large meeting—an audience of more than 1,000 church pastors. And before that group, the leaders began to criticize me, hoping I would start a fight. During that time the Holy Spirit really was with me. So I just stood in front of the pulpit with a smile. And while they cried out their slogans, I sensed a heavenly peace deep down in my heart.

DKN: Was it tempting to want to give in? I mean, over a thousand pastors! Did you feel, "Well, maybe I ought to make a little compromise this one time?"

WONG: No, because during that time I really felt I wanted to stand for Jesus and for the truth I had discovered in Him. And what is so wonderful is that I later learned that at least two of those 1,000 pastors left that place, studied the Scriptures for themselves, and accepted Jesus as Lord of the Sabbath, too!

DKN: All because of your loyal witness! But in the meantime the communist government began to crack down further, and six years later you ended up in prison. What happened?

WONG: During those six years I worked in the underground church. But finally I was caught. For keeping my faith and preaching the Gospel, I was sentenced to jail and a compulsory hard labor camp.

DKN: It was a short sentence?

WONG: My first four years were spent in maximum security, totally isolated from my family and the community. No letters out, no letters in. Imprisoned alone. Then after the first four years, there was for some reason a change in policy. And I was moved into one of the formal prison cells, and letter writing privileges were granted me.

DKN: How often could you write home?

WONG: The new policy said that I could send one letter a month. And the letter had to be limited to 100 Chinese characters.

DKN: Only a single letter per month. Any family visits?

WONG: Yes, once a month two family members were allowed to visit me for eight minutes. And let me tell you, those eight minutes seemed like eight seconds. Soon the guard would be standing there barking, "Time's up." And I would be led back to my cell.

DKN: Well, at least you had all your books with you so you could study the Scriptures and keep your mind active.

WONG: Oh, no! During that time we were not allowed to have a bed, chair, desk, or books of any kind. The only book I was allowed to read as a prisoner was called the Red Bible—a collection of Chairman Mao's quotations. I longed for a Bible—a real Bible. But that was not to be.

DKN: Until you thought of a plan.

WONG: That, I feel, was God's miraculous gift for me. When I wrote the first letter, at first I wanted the family to send me some food. But above all I desperately needed a copy of the Bible. Even though I could remember many Bible verses and share with others, I still wanted to have the Bible with me. But how could I communicate this to my family? Not only was it very dangerous, but also not many copies of the Bible were left in the community. But just at that time I heard a voice on the upper floor of the prison. It was one of the guards calling a prisoner's identification number. "Prisoner number 115, number 115." And suddenly the Holy Spirit enlightened my mind and helped me to remember that number 115 in our old Chinese hymnal was, "Give Me the Bible."

So I quickly decided to use that number and added one more line to my short letter: "Please send me a *115*-page notebook." I emphasized 115. Then, with a sincere prayer, I handed my letter to the guard, because before we could mail the letter, they checked it carefully. I was praying hard that they would not discover my sacred secret!

DKN: What is phenomenal to me is that your sister got hold of this letter, saw the number 115, recalled the same hymn, and knew what you are asking! That's what is truly incredible.

WONG: I fully believe the same Spirit who enlightened my mind also gave my family members understanding and insight to learn my thinking.

DKN: So here came the next once-a-month, eight-minute visit with your family. They brought you their little goodies—and, by the way, the guard had to check all that they brought?

WONG: Sure.

DKN: Did your heart fall when you saw in those goodies nothing but what—a bar of soap and maybe some food?

WONG: Yes. At first I didn't know what they had sent to me, but just before the visitation was over, my sister whispered to me, "Robert, when you use the laundry soap, cut it into two pieces." I nodded my head with an understanding smile.

DKN: All right, Bob, now look, for the sake of those of us who use tiny bars of soap, obviously this wasn't Ivory or Dial soap. What size was it?

WONG: It was a huge bar of soap.

DKN: So you went humming "Give Me the Bible" all the way back to the cell. Because by this time your faith believed that your prayers had been answered inside that large bar of soap. But what about your cellmates? Wouldn't they find out?

WONG: It was very difficult. You know, once they found something strange, they had to report it. So in the evening when darkness came into our small cell, I turned my back to my cellmates and put some dirty clothes into a basin to soak them. Then I broke the bar in half, and there was a pocket New Testament wrapped in plastic paper. So I got it.

DKN: You got it, indeed! But Robert, from 1964 to 1979 you were imprisoned: solitary confinement. Then followed an extended prison sentence, and finally hard labor. Finally in 1979, word came of the normalization of U.S. and Chinese relations. Prisoners were freed. And you left your homeland. But is the story over? Looking back over the high price you paid for that kind of loyalty to Jesus, I must ask you in closing what was it, what is it that fuels your allegiance to God?

WONG: I really feel the Lord Jesus Christ loves me so much that I could not deny Him or not hold high His name, especially among so many people in China. They really do not have a chance to know Christ and His truth. I have felt God calling me to give my life for Him in my country. So for me, when I arrived in the States, even though some people urged me, "You are better to find another job or take some medical technology to be a self-supporting minister," I simply could not. How can I do anything but share the Good News of Jesus?

In China I did not have the freedom to preach. Even so I was put in the jail. Now I enjoy freedom here, and I can share what I have found in Jesus. But I want to return to my people. God has been my reason for living, and I believe He will open the door for me to share the truth about the Lord of Salvation, Who is the Lord of the Sabbath, with my homeland.

❖ ❖ ❖ ❖

A prison cell in China or your neighborhood back at home. The apocalyptic truth is still the same, is it not? Because if the only loyalty worth living for is a loyalty that's worth dying for, isn't it equally true that *a loyalty worth dying for is the only loyalty worth living for?* So what are we waiting for? Loyalty to the Lamb—or loyalty to Lucifer? It is our call—it is our choice.

REVELATION 16:13-15; 7:9, 13, 14

And I saw three foul spirits like frogs coming from the mouth of the dragon, from the mouth of the beast, and from the mouth of the false prophet.

These are demonic spirits, performing signs, who go abroad to the kings of the whole world, to assemble them for battle on the great day of God the Almighty.

("See, I am coming like a thief! Blessed is the one who stays awake and is clothed, not going about naked and exposed to shame.")

After this I looked, and there was a great multitude that no one could count, from every nation, from all tribes and peoples and languages, standing before the throne and before the Lamb, robed in white, with palm branches in their hands.

Then one of the elders addressed me, saying "Who are these, robed in white, and where have they come from?"

I said to him, "Sir, you are the one that knows." Then he said to me, "These are they who have come out of the great ordeal; they have washed their robes and made them white in the blood of the Lamb."

5

Showdown of the Gods

Dial 911

Isn't it true that we live in a world where 911 has become the most popular phone number around? A few months ago the *Los Angeles Times* published a list of "emergencies" that the LA Fire Department dispatchers radioed to emergency medical crews for response. Actually, these emergency calls weren't really emergencies—they were "no sends," as the dispatchers used to call them. But because of a lawsuit over a tragic mistake in 1987, all "no sends" have been eliminated. It is now the law in Los Angeles that every call to 911 be treated as a real emergency. Here are some of the calls the crews have been required to race to since then (as recorded by the dispatchers):

❑ Eighteen-year-old male can't get rest at home, wants ride to hospital.

- ❏ Man in blue cowboy hat and yellow pants has swollen feet.

- ❏ Sixty-one-year-old woman is worried because her stomach is not growling.

- ❏ Person answered "No" to question "Are you conscious?" (The question is more intriguing than the answer!)

- ❏ Lady has blisters on her feet from working for three days at Taco Bell.

- ❏ "This guy is inside Humphrey Medical Center" (reports the dispatcher). Says the people inside are not helping him fast enough, so he called 911. (A rather original idea for the next time the nurse takes too long to answer your call button!)

- ❏ Twenty-two-year-old says half of his face is asleep. (I've had a few students whose *entire* faces were asleep during one of my lectures!)

- ❏ Out of breath from "running from the police."

Unbelievable emergency calls! And yet it is true, isn't it, that we live in a world where 911 has become the most operative phone number around? So welcome to the 911 age of human civilization, when it seems we keep waking up each morning to another global crisis. A time when all the presidential elections in the world will never be able to produce a human leader who can solve the mounting economic and ecological, monetary and moral dilemmas that threaten us. A time when, if you believe the black Book on your shelf, we are accelerating toward the end of all civilization.

One irrefutable fact of life these days is that we all live in a world terrorized by the enemy of the universe. For that reason we keep returning to the dusty Apocalypse, where we find the divine exposé of Lucifer's final and desperate strategy to sweep our entire planet into his black bastion.

Consider for a moment history's final 911 call before the return of the King, Christ Jesus. What is so unsettling is the realization that what the Apocalypse describes here is already in place. All that remains is for someone to dial the numbers.

Three Frogs

> And I saw three foul spirits like frogs coming from the mouth of the dragon, from the mouth of the beast, and from the mouth of the false prophet. These are demonic spirits, performing signs, who go abroad to the kings of the whole world, to assemble them for battle on the great day of God the Almighty (Revelation 16:13, 14).

Three foul and froggish spirits, crawling from the mouths of the dragon, the beast, and the false prophet. And as Revelation 16:15 notes ("See, I am coming like a thief!"), all of this happens just before the return of Christ. What under heaven is going on now?

One thing is certain: In this threefold end-time union, we have a new trinity—a new, dark triumvirate. And who should be at all surprised? For we remember that Lucifer, the fallen angelic rebel—here again symbolized by a dragon—has always hungered to be like God. Failing to usurp the divine throne in heaven and then being expelled to the earth, do you think for a moment that he would forget his dream? Not on your life—or his! "I will make myself like the Most High" (Isaiah 14:12). "So I, too," he says, "shall have my trinity: the dragon, the beast, and the false prophet." Thus, with his own fallen mind, Lucifer snares two other end-time powers to join himself in forming a trinity—a demonic trinity. And who are these other two powers?

The Beast Again

The beast John writes of is, as noted in previous chapters of this book, the first beast power of Revelation 13's first ten verses. The internal evidence is irrefutable, as we established earlier, that this beast power is a religio-political power that exercised mighty dominance during the historical period of the Christian Church known as the Dark or Middle Ages. Over 1,200 years of its domination is suddenly and mysteriously ended when, in the apocalyptic scenario, this religio-political power is wounded, taken captive, and nearly disappears from history. But then, just as mysteriously, its mortal wound is healed, and this beast power reclaims geo-religio-political dominance on earth.

Only one power throughout the history of Christendom can possibly match this apocalyptic description: the Roman papacy. But once again I must add that John is describing a power and not a person, an institution and not an individual, a system and not a soul.

A few weeks ago I had the privilege of baptizing a Roman Catholic businessman who, like millions of other Catholics, has lived as a sincere Christian follower of God. There is not a single person in that church who matches this apocalyptic description, but there is an institution that does. The millions of martyrs during the Dark and Middle Ages are mute testimony to a powerful institution that will not tolerate for long any conscience that chooses to disregard her authority. And she is on the rise again, with breathtaking rapidity.

Consider the dispatch from the August 25, 1991, issue of London's *The Sunday Telegraph,* as noted in *Light* magazine—a monthly English religious journal:

> Europe's new emperor? With European 'federalism' on the agenda of both Western and Eastern governments, speculations are abroad as to who may become the political leader of the united European Community. A profile in the "Sunday Comment" of *The Sunday Telegraph* on John Paul II is suggesting that he is the best choice in the new Holy European Empire. The article speaks of the increasing role of the Roman Catholic political power since the fall of Napoleon and even since the

counter Reformation. The moral authority of the papacy becomes the apparent winner of the day. "If European federalism triumphs, the EC will indeed be an empire. It will lack an emperor; but it will have the Pope. It is difficult not to think that Wojtyla realizes this," *The Sunday Telegraph* suggests. (*Light*, December, 1991)

The False Prophet

But there are *three* powers in this new end-time trinity—the dragon, the beast, and the false prophet. The dragon and the beast, we know, but who is this false prophet? We have not encountered him yet in the Apocalypse. However, a quick check reveals beyond question who this power is. Notice how Revelation 19:20 speaks of this new trinity's destruction at the return of Christ: "And the beast was captured, and with it the false prophet who had performed in its presence the signs by which he deceived those that had received the mark of the beast."

Signs in the presence of the first beast? That rings an apocalyptic bell, for did we not read such a description in chapter 13, too? "[The second beast power] performs great signs, even making fire come down from heaven to earth in the sight of all; and by the signs that it is allowed to perform on behalf of the [first] beast, it deceives the inhabitants of earth, telling them to make an image for the beast that had been wounded by the sword and yet lived" (Revelation 13:13, 14).

Clearly, "the false prophet" is but another appellation for the second beast of chapter 13. And who is the second beast? Again, as our previous chapters have noted, it is that power that sprang up in human history at the very time the first beast was wounded in 1798, when its pope was taken captive by Napoleon. According to that prophecy, this second power, born in the late 1700s far from the crossroads of Europe, would one day enjoy sole, global superpower status. Arising in the late 1700s, far from Europe, and a global superpower in the end . . . there is only one power on earth that matches this apocalyptic description. And that is the United States of America.

It is also vitally significant, as noted in Chapter 4, that the Apocalypse depicts both powers achieving their global dominance at the same time, peaking together at the end of time. And according to the prophecy, the second power will become the key player in leading the entire earth to worship the first beast power.

Enter now the February 24, 1992, issue of *Time* magazine. In its cover story and title is the sobering vindication of this apocalyptic prophecy. "Holy Alliance" the bold title proclaims. Subtitle: "How Reagan and the Pope conspired to assist Poland's Solidarity movement and hasten the demise of Communism: An Investigative Report." For the first time the nation and world have learned, through the investigative reporting of the renowned journalist Carl Bernstein, that in a private meeting in the Vatican Library on Monday, June 7, 1982, "Reagan and the Pope agreed to undertake a clandestine campaign to hasten the dissolution of the communist empire" (p. 28).

Their strategy was to work through the cooperative efforts of the Central Intelligence Agency and the Roman Catholic Church, behind the front of the Solidarity labor union. They intended to drive a dagger into the belly of the Bear, and through the collapse of communism in Poland, achieve the demise of communism in the world. Both leaders knew that communism stood between them and global domination. So they joined forces.

Listen to how Richard Allen, Reagan's first National Security Adviser, described this new union: "'This was one of the great secret alliances of all time.'" (p. 28) Oh, no, Mr. Allen, it was no secret at all! Nineteen hundred years earlier, God sent an apocalyptic prophecy predicting that these two self-same powers would form an end-time holy alliance—the very title the *Time* editors chose for their investigative report. Allen, himself a Roman Catholic, further described the bond of unity the pope and the president shared: "'a unity of spiritual view and a unity of vision on the Soviet empire: that right or correctness would ultimately prevail in the divine plan'" (p. 30).

Prevailing in the divine plan? It would better be phrased as "prevailing in the divine *prophecy*"! We see a "holy alliance" that collaborates in shattering history and writing incredible new headlines. "Step by reluctant step, the Soviets and the communist government of Poland bowed to the moral, economic, and political pressure imposed by the Pope and the President" (p. 35). The moral and economic and political pressure imposed by these two global superpowers? Why, it is as if someone were reading off the cue sheets of Revelation 13! "Holy Alliance," the prestigious international newsweekly calls it! And who can be surprised? What we are witnessing today in this newly disclosed ten-year-old secret (which certainly makes one wonder what else might be going on at this very moment that we have yet to learn of) is the breathtaking unfolding of what Jesus, through John, declared would be a sign of the impending end.

The Dragon Again

But in the end, chapter 16 declares, there will be a *threefold* union, not simply a twofold holy alliance. So enter now the third partner—the nether world, the gray and black regions of the demonic dragon.

New Age? No, a very, very Old Age—in fact, an age-old deception called spiritism or spiritualism. The pagan cultures of history have been riddled with demonic infiltration. But alas, the Christian culture of an end-time world will likewise become possessed. And it is through this third partner that the kings of the world, the great cultures of humankind, will at last be united.

After I had begun writing this book, I received a very informative paper from one of the economics professors at Andrews University, Charles Stokes. He reminded me that the eastern half of this globe must figure into the Apocalypse somewhere. America and Rome are not the only playing fields for the dragon's last stand. Eastern religions must emerge in the apocalyptic plot somewhere. And of course, he is right. And here is the somewhere. The New Age-Old Age-somewhere of eastern mysticism, animism, and spiritism. Here is where, in the apocalyptic scenario, there is a trifold union. And in the end, paganism and Christianity are both taken captive by the dragon of demonism.

> And I saw three foul spirits like frogs coming from the mouth of the dragon, from the mouth of the beast, and from the mouth of the false prophet. these are demonic spirits, performing signs, who go abroad to the kings of the whole world, to assemble them for battle on the great day of God the Almighty. (Revelation 16:13,14)

Christianity taken captive by demonism? Impossible! you say. Consider the mounting evidence carefully.

Pontifex Maximus

First, consider this piece of history. In the early years of western civilization, the high priest of a pagan cult adopted a title that became a symbol of his contact and communion with the gods. It was a simple title, and it simply meant: "The Greatest Bridge Builder."

In Latin, "greatest" is *maximus;* "bridge" is *pons;* and "builder" comes from *factio,* which means "I make." "The Greatest Bridge Builder," or in Latin, *Pontifex Maximus.*

In A.D. 375, the Christian emperor, Gratian, ascended to the throne of the Roman Empire and refused the pagan vestments and pagan title that Roman emperors had received as head of the pagan cult of the empire. But while the emperor refused the title, the bishop of Rome eventually embraced it as a symbol of his own ecclesiastical dignity and status and in effect replaced the high priest of paganism as the new bridge builder. So it is that a pagan title born of the nether world—The Greatest Bridge

Builder—is still claimed by the Bishop of Rome: *Pontifex Maximus*. And very much a bridge-builder this apocalyptic power has proven to be!

The Apparition

Come with me to a crowded village chapel. It is 5:40 p.m. in Medjugorje, Yugoslavia. What you're about to witness has been taking place daily since June 24, 1981. All eyes are focused on the two young women kneeling in the choir loft, their stares fixed on a blank wall, lips moving in silent prayer. Finally they arise and emerge, "with a new message from Our Lady of Medjugorje urging a deeper devotion to her Son and closer attention to peace, prayers and penance" (*US News and World Report,* March 12, 1990, p. 67).

What has just transpired? What is it that has drawn eleven million pilgrims (many from the United States, Canada, and Australia) to this obscure village in Yugoslavia? It is what is now being called a "Marian Apparition." The two women believe that Mary, the mother of Christ, appears to them every day at that time and in that place, with a message for the world. Father Guiseppe Besutti, professor at Rome's Pontifical Marianum School, says the church cannot afford simply to ignore the apparitions. After all, he says, "The church itself is founded on an apparition—that of Christ resurrected" (*Ibid.*).

The Vatican itself acknowledges a "surprising increase" in recent years in claims of presumed apparitions, visions, and messages associated with Mary. French theologian René Laurentin, widely recognized as an expert in Marian theology, counts more than 200 such events since 1930 (interestingly enough, this begins with the year after the healing of Catholicism's wound in 1929).

What's going on? Lubbock, Texas; Ambridge, Pennsylvania; Lourdes, France; Fatima, Portugal; Guadalupe, Mexico. But then, should we be surprised? Not when Lucifer's primeval lie to Eve in the Garden was, "You will not die" (Genesis 3:4). You don't die when you die, he says: you go to heaven or to hell or to purgatory; but you don't go to sleep as the Bible teaches. This has been Lucifer's lie from the very pristine beginning. The immortality of the human soul has not a contextual shred of evidence in the entire Scriptures. It simply is a lie. And Lucifer knows it.

The "soul" and "spirit" of human beings are referred to over 1,700 times in the Bible but are never once said to be immortal or eternal. In fact, the Bible clearly states that only God is immortal (1 Timothy 6:14-16). The spirit that returns to God at death is not a conscious entity, but is the breath of life (Ecclesiastes 12:7; Genesis 2:7). The words *spirit, wind,* and *breath* in our English translations come from the same original Hebrew and Greek words in the Bible.

The Bible says the dead cannot remember or give thanks (Psalm 6:5), cannot praise God (Psalm 115:17; Isaiah 38:18), cannot think (Psalm 146:3, 4), and cannot function (Ecclesiastes 9:5, 6, 10). Their abode is the grave, not heaven (Acts 2:29, 34). Thus Jesus referred to death as sleep, as did other Bible prophets over seventy times (see John 11:11-14).

In the light of this irrefutable biblical evidence, we would do well then to heed the apocalyptic warning: "These are demonic spirits, performing signs" (Revelation 16:14). A power is evident on earth today that is indeed the greatest bridge builder of all time between the dark nether world and the Christian Church. Therefore it is neither coincidental nor accidental that the world today is experiencing a massive barrage of Marian apparitions—ghost-like appearances supposedly of the mother of Jesus—who keep sending messages to this planet. But in light of media headlines, we must ask ourselves where these messages are coming from. If the Bible is true when it teaches that at death we enter the sleep of death and await the resurrection, then Mary herself is awaiting the resurrection. So again—where are these messages coming from? Could they be coming from one whose dark passion has from the beginning been to sweep the entire planet into his fated bastion?

Consider now *Time* magazine's cover story for December

30, 1991: "Mary: Handmaid or Feminist?" (By the way, if you're noticing that *Time* carries a preponderance of reports regarding Roman Catholicism, you have only to remember that its founder, Henry Luce, was married to Clare Booth Luce, the playwright and politician, who, after their marriage, converted to Catholicism. Editorially, this magazine continues to reflect contemporary American Catholicism.)

Read a few lines from this cover story and ponder their implications for a moment:

> When he was made a bishop in 1958, John Paul emblazoned a golden *M* on his coat of arms and chose as his Latin motto *"Totus Tuus"* (All Yours)—*referring to Mary, not Christ.* Once he put on St. Peter's ring, John Paul made Mary's unifying power a centerpiece of his papal arsenal. He has visited countless Marian shrines during his globe trotting, and invokes the Madonna's aid in nearly every discourse and prayer that he delivers. He firmly believes that her personal intercession spared his life when he was shot at in St. Peter's Square in Rome in 1981; the assassination attempt occurred on May 13, the exact anniversary of the first Fatima apparition [a 1917 "appearance" of Mary to three Portuguese children, the notoriety of which still draws a steady 4.5 million pilgrims a year from around the world to Fatima].
>
> Moreover, John Paul is firmly convinced, as are many others, that Mary brought an end to communism throughout Europe. His faith is rooted in the famed prophecies of Mary at Fatima in 1917. According to Sister Lucia, one of the children who claimed to see her, the Virgin predicted the rise of Soviet totalitarianism before it happened. In a subsequent vision, she directed the Pope and his bishops to consecrate Russia to her Immaculate Heart in order to bring communism to an end.

> According to Lucia, papal attempts to carry out that consecration failed in 1942, '52 and '82. John Paul finally carried out Mary's directive correctly in 1984—and the very next year Mikhail Gorbachev's rise to power inaugurated the Soviet collapse. Says Father Robert Fox of the Fatima Family Shrine in Alexandria, S. Dak.: "The world will recognize in due time that *the defeat of communism came at the intercession of the mother of Jesus."* (pp. 64, 65, emphasis supplied)

Add to that Malachi Martin's firm contention that while he was convalescing after the assassination attempt, John Paul II experienced "nothing less than a personal communication from Heaven." "It was in this mode of prayer and this mood of total trust in Mary that John Paul had what has been, as far as is publicly known, his only supernatural vision of things to come. There is no gainsaying that he did have that vision" (*The Keys of This Blood,* pp. 48, 627).

A New Spirit?

Spirits and apparitions in the heart of Rome. Is it any different in the heart of the United States? Just ask Hollywood, which in 1991 alone produced a dozen after-life movies, including "Ghost" which netted $500 million globally in its first year. One reviewer calls it Hollywood's new fascination with "necrophilic romance." Lovers who don't really die—they just hang around in thin air! Funny, funny, and oh, how captivating! Brilliant, really, if you're the dragon who has dispatched your demonic spirits to deceive the entire world into believing your falsehood that when you die, you don't really die.

Listen to Larry Gordon, chief executive of the movie production company Largo Entertainment: "We all want to believe that death isn't so bad" (*Time,* June 3, 1991, p. 70). Which is precisely what the serpent hissed in Eden! As one reviewer put it: "The Grim Reaper and the fires of hell have been slickly supplanted by a blissful feel-good death in the form of reincarnation. Dying is depicted as a transitory state, at worst a move to a new neighborhood" (*Ibid.*). How did the Apocalypse put it? "These are demonic spirits performing signs."

And yes, I fear that United States Protestantism is being led down the same primrose pathway.

For part of my doctoral studies, I attended a seminary on the west coast. I was invited one evening to sit in on a seminary class called "Signs and Wonders." The instructor was a popular charismatic pastor and preacher. The thrust of the class was to encourage supernatural wonders in the parishes of the pastors taking the class, and thus facilitate growth and ministry in those parishes. When the class ended late that evening, the pastor-professor began to exercise his supernatural gift and began to call out ailments and illnesses that he saw in his mind's eye. And as he did so, the class began to pray for individuals who raised their hands and said, "Yes, I'm the one with that back pain," or "Yes, I do have a stomach problem," or "Yes, I'm the one you were just shown, and I do have that very disease."

Signs and wonders, indeed! It's a billion-dollar television industry now for evangelical Christianity in this land. Pat Robertson can—in front of the TV camera—pray a hurricane away from the Carolina coast. Superpower faith healers can heal before your very eyes. And while skeptical news analysts can attempt to expose fraud or sleight of hand, the fact remains that through the tidal wave of charismatic pentecostalism in this nation today, Americans are being swept into a desperate counterfeit of miracles and tongues and other such supernatural manifestations. And like the Marian apparitions, these manifestations are subtly, quietly setting people up for the final, overpowering delusion Lucifer has reserved for this planet (and which I am compelled to share with you in the next chapter).

Protestantism, Catholicism, and spiritism? Even months ago, who would ever have believed such a silent and secret confederacy to be possible? And yet the very press that reports our daily headlines now chronicles a mysterious global onslaught of apparitions. The occult, with its slick Madison Avenue, New Age front—and with Shirley MacLaine as its high priestess—has already possessed the entertainment industry (television and theater) including the once-revered Walt Disney film productions. (A quick review of Disney's most recent films will startle you with its unabashed preoccupation with the supernatural and the occult.)

And what about the widely acclaimed and syndicated horoscope columns in the major newspapers of this nation? Apparently these horoscopes even made believers out of the former President and First Lady of the United States, so that Ronald Reagan's official itinerary was carefully plotted by an astrologer's consultation with the planets and stars! And what shall be said of Lucifer's subliminal battering of minds through the sensational predictions of supermarket psychics that taunt every grocery shopper in this nation? Are we being set up?

Inescapable is the conclusion that somebody has masterminded a dark strategy to snare an entire civilization, Christian and pagan, Western and Eastern, First World and Third World, educated and illiterate, rich and poor. A brilliant but dark strategy—and a new trinity for a final, desperate coalition. The Apocalypse declares that such evidence is an unmistakable sign of the impending end. Listen to these words:

> When Protestantism shall stretch her hand across
> the gulf to grasp the hand of the Roman power,
> when she shall reach over the abyss to clasp hands
> with spiritualism, when, under the influence of
> this threefold union, our country shall repudiate
> every principle of its Constitution as a Protestant
> and republican government . . . then we may know
> that the time has come for the marvelous working
> of Satan and that the end is near (*Testimonies for the
> Church*, Vol. 5, p. 451).

A Strategy for Survival

Two cover stories in two months—and a pulsating piece

of the Apocalypse—both declare: The end is much nearer than we first thought. Does it frighten you—scare you? It doesn't have to, because I have discovered how to survive the fury of this demonic end-run.

John saw the survivors and heard their secret in Revelation 7:13, 14:

> Then one of the elders addressed me, saying, "Who are these, robed in white, and where have they come from?" I said to him, "Sir, you are the one that knows." Then he said to me, "These are they who have come out of the great ordeal; they have washed their robes and made them white in the blood of the Lamb."

They will be a people who have learned to daily, fervently dial 911 to the Christ of Calvary. In fact, so intense is their desire to live for Him that they are described as washing their lives in His life-giving blood.

Has not the time come at last for that very intensity in your life and mine? A time to saturate our days and our lives in the crimson of a living, dynamic friendship with the Lord of Calvary, the Lamb of heaven—the very One who taught us how to pray, "Our Father, who is in heaven . . . deliver us from evil"? He taught us the quiet and trusting prayer that in God's friendship we have been given all the deliverance we shall ever need. And no demonic trinity shall ever be able to snatch us from Him who is our eternity!

So what are we waiting for? How much stronger must Lucifer's coalition become before we pursue this apocalyptic intensity with Jesus? Does it not occur to you that if we wait any longer, it may be too late?

REVELATION 3:14-22

And to the angel of the church in Laodicea write: The words of the Amen, the faithful and true witness, the original of God's creation:

"I know your works; you are neither cold nor hot. So, because you are lukewarm, and neither cold nor hot, I am about to spit you out of my mouth. For you say, 'I am rich, I have prospered, and I need nothing.' You do not realize that you are wretched, pitiable, poor, blind, and naked. Therefore I counsel you to buy from me gold refined by fire so that you may be rich; and white robes to clothe you and to keep the shame of your nakedness from being seen; and salve to anoint your eyes so that you may see. I reprove and discipline those whom I love. Be earnest, therefore, and repent. Listen! I am standing at the door, knocking; if you hear my voice and open the door, I will come in to you and eat with you, and you with me. To the one who conquers I will give a place with me on my throne, just as I myself conquered and sat down with my Father on his throne. Let anyone who has an ear listen to what the Spirit is saying to the churches."

6

When the Heat's on Hot

Michelangelo

Did you know that Michelangelo was born in 1992? And that because he was, the world was nearly turned upside down? If you're only a history buff and not a computer whiz, then you're already sure something's wrong with such a declaration, since history buffs and art connoisseurs all know that Michelangelo was born on March 6, 1475—not 1992.

But computer whizzes and hacks all know that Michelangelo was born on March 6, 1992. That's Michelangelo the virus, not Michelangelo the artist! Michelangelo the computer virus—which struck right on schedule, March 6, 1992. And thanks to this ingenious and secret electronic virus, thousands upon thousands of computers worldwide were reported to have been affected, tainted, and "diseased." But as a result of all the advance press on the anticipated attack, most computers, including ours at the Pioneer Memorial Church, were de-virused in time.

But Michelangelo did strike our campus! According to one of our resident computer specialists, the Seminary was hit first. But then, I wasn't surprised. Since Michelangelo the artist did so much religious artwork, it is no wonder that Michelangelo the virus chose the Seminary first!

Actually, industry authorities tell us that there are now over 1,200 computer viruses circulating around the world. And they behave just like biological viruses, rapidly reproducing themselves as they strike. Their creators? Mad hackers somewhere who design an electronic series of commands that can infiltrate an unsuspecting computer or piece of hardware and eventually destroy the files stored in that electronic memory bank—the hard disk.

Sinister viruses designed to infiltrate and destroy the world of computers. Sound familiar? For hasn't the history of this planet been plagued with an enemy virus conceived in the heart of one who has always wanted to be, not Michelangelo, but Michael the Archangel (Revelation 12:7)? So desperate was Lucifer's passion that it got him thrown out of heaven for his viral attack. But never mind heaven. This counterfeit Michael, known better as Satan or the Devil, has planted his destroying virus deep within the human system on earth. And one day soon—mark these words—the right date will come, the virus will activate, and humanity will be thrown into total chaos—deceived and destroyed on the day when Lucifer appears as Michael.

The Last Temptation

In the cryptic words of a single line from the Apocalypse, the horrible truth emerges: "They worshiped the dragon" (Revelation 13:4). You know what that means, don't you? It means that Lucifer's last dream will at last come true. The very dream he bartered over with Jesus in that foodless, barren wilderness, when he hissed: "I will give You the entire planet, all the kingdoms of the world, if You will bow down and worship me." (See Matthew 4:9.) No suffering, no death, no sacrifice, no pain—if You will simply bow down and call me "Lord," You can have it all.

Lucifer has never forgotten that offer. And if Jesus refused it, then too bad. For there will be a planet in the end that will take it—hook, line, and sinker. So mark these words well within your own soul: It will come to this planet—that wilderness temptation—one last time. It will be earth's final, searing test. It will be the overmastering delusion. And it will come, just as surely as Revelation 13:4 is in your Bible.

And just what is it that will come? Put two verses together in your mind, and then you will know for yourself what will come. "And no wonder! Even Satan disguises himself as an angel of light" (2 Corinthians 11:14). And one more: "These are demonic spirits, performing signs, who go abroad to the kings of the whole world" (Revelation 16:14). But then for good measure, let me add a third verse—the warning of Jesus in Matthew 24:24: "For false messiahs [or Christs] will appear and produce great signs and omens, to lead astray, if possible, even the elect."

The last deception—the overmastering delusion. What will it be? It will certainly be more than the small boxed ad I read in the newspaper the other day: "Jesus is back! Jesus has returned to Earth and is presenting THE WHITE CROSS as the symbol for Christianity. The WHITE CROSS removes Jesus from the cross and puts the light of God where it should be. Receive a FREE pocket size copy of The WHITE CROSS and a prayer sheet from Jesus. Send a stamped self addressed envelope to: Church of the Second Coming . . . ." And then an address in Chicago was given. While this peculiar advertisement may qualify as an aberrant fulfillment of the prediction Jesus made long ago about false Christs, it is hardly on the scale of an end-time Luciferian attack!

Instead, logically applying the three verses we noted above, it is not difficult to imagine what the enemy's overmastering final temptation will be like.

I picture internationally known newscasters there—the likes of Dan Rather, Tom Brokaw, and Peter Jennings. There they are that day with all their high-tech hardware. Their satellite trucks are parked bumper to bumper all over the boulevard and sidewalks, right up to the foot of the capitol stairs. Technicians are practically falling over each other in their efforts to quickly secure their electronic cables and uplink signals. Giant television cameras, their ON-AIR red lights flashing, begin to zoom in with their unblinking glass eyes upon the most spectacular display of demonic deception ever witnessed on earth. For there he is, perhaps hovering a few feet off the ground—a being of dazzling light and shimmering glory. A mysterious guest from the unseen world who, with the light of a blazing sun, today appears in the capital of the world's last superpower—the United States. CNN and every other news network is covering this stupendous moment live.

One by one, senators and representatives arrive in their tailored suits. They line up and down the marbled capitol stairs. The Supreme Court justices are present, garbed in their black regal attire. Why, it is as if Washington's power elite were congregated for yet another State of the Union address by the President. But in fact, what they will hear today is a State of the Planet address by the being atop the stairway.

Also lining the capitol steps are the most well-known and popular religious leaders of the nation. Faces that have become familiar nationwide, thanks to their many years of appearing on America's TV screens. Eloquent, charismatic, acclaimed, they too have received their summons to rendezvous with this moment in eternity.

Crowds choke Pennsylvania Avenue and are sprawled across the Capitol Mall. Thousands have converged upon the nation's capital to witness this unprecedented moment of history, everyone craning for a glimpse of promised glory.

A black limousine escorted by a flashing motorcade of police cars and motorcycles pulls up to the capitol stairs. The doors swing open, and the President of the United States emerges. A popular take-charge leader himself, there is a timidity and hesitancy noticeable on his face as the cameras of the world record his steps toward the being atop the stairs. As thousands of video cams pan the scene and point up the stairway, the light becomes so intense that the cameras keep bleeding to total white on their monitors, their F-stops closed down.

The majestic being smiles at the approaching president, and thanks to CNN, the whole world gazes upon this breathtaking moment. "Welcome, my son! I have waited for you; I have come for you. Welcome to all my children on this planet." The being needs no cue to turn and gaze fully into the ON-AIR cameras pointed at him. "Welcome, for my father sends you his peace and his love. I come from my father and your father; I promised I would come; you prayed I would come; and now at last I am here. My peace I leave with you; my peace I give to you."

What appear to be nail-scarred hands are lifted into the air; and, as if on cue, the legislators, the president, the press, the masses choking the boulevards, all bow down and worship the returned Christ. "Christ has come!" Like a mighty roar the cry ascends to heaven.

Listen to how that prescient book *The Great Controversy* describes the moment:

> As the crowning act in the great drama of deception, Satan himself will personate Christ. [The verses we noted a moment ago are proof enough!] The church has long professed to look to the Saviour's advent as the consummation of her hopes. Now the great deceiver will make it appear that Christ has come. In different parts of the earth, Satan will manifest himself among men as a majestic being of dazzling brightness, resembling the description of the Son of God given by John in the Revelation. Revelation 1:13-15. The glory that surrounds him is unsurpassed by anything that mortal eyes have yet beheld. The shout of triumph rings

out upon the air: 'Christ has come! Christ has come!' The people prostrate themselves in adoration before him, while he lifts up his hands and pronounces a blessing upon them, as Christ blessed His disciples when He was upon the earth. His voice is soft and subdued, yet full of melody. In gentle, compassionate tones he presents some of the same gracious heavenly truths which the Saviour uttered; he heals the diseases of the people, and then, in his assumed character of Christ, he claims to have changed the Sabbath to Sunday, and commands all to hallow the day which he has blessed. He declares that those who persist in keeping holy the seventh day are blaspheming his name by refusing to listen to his angels sent to them with light and truth. This is the strong, almost overmastering delusion (p. 624).

"They worshiped the dragon, for he had given his authority to the beast, and they worshiped the beast, saying, 'Who is like the beast, and who can fight against it?'"

There are two powers in Revelation 13, you remember. And you can be utterly certain that at the basilica of the other power, the impersonating Christ will also appear. In fact, the entire planet will be hailing Lucifer as Lord. His dream at last will have come true.

They're Waiting

The headline from the March 8, 1992, edition of the *Chicago Tribune* would have caught the eye of anyone reading the Apocalypse these days: "Jewish sect convinced Messiah's arrival is near." Dateline: Kfar Habad, Israel. I went on to read:

After a year that witnessed the fall of Soviet communism and the emergence of a new world order, it seems only prudent to consider the possibility of something really big happening—like the coming of the Messiah. A large and influential segment of

Israel's ultraorthodox Jewish community is convinced the moment is at hand. In recent days, billboards and bumper stickers announcing the
Messiah's imminent arrival have sprouted throughout the country. Many believers have mounted
small Day-Glo signs atop their cars to herald the
event.

They believe their Messiah is soon to come. And putting
to shame some of our own less-than-enthusiastic anticipation
of the event, look how they are unashamedly announcing the
impending day!

According to Rabbi Menachem Brod, a spokesman
for [this sect of Jews in Israel], the Talmudic sages
have always said the Messiah's coming will be pre-
ceded by a long period of darkness and confusion.
[Sound familiar?] "We now know that period has
been the last 70 years. We have been through two
world wars, the collapse of communism. There has
never before been such a period of hardship and
change," Brod said. "It's like the game kids play
where you connect the dots and gradually the
whole picture is revealed. Events examined indi-
vidually don't look like much, but when you connect the dots, you see the meaning."

Which is precisely what the Apocalypse has been trying
to tell us! But of all places, we read it in the Sunday paper,
where we run into a Jewish sect that has connected the dots
of current events and discovered the sign of a soon-coming
Messiah! So fervent is their conviction that, according to this
article, "many have taken to wearing phone beepers with a
special number that will let them know the moment the
Messiah arrives."

But while we quickly commend how they've integrated
their hopes into their daily lives, still, their very story gives
one pause for reflection. For would it not be entirely consis-
tent with Lucifer's end-time strategy to counterfeit the hope

of all the great religions of this world? And would it not logically follow that it is very possible—even probable—that the deceiver of the human race would appear to all the religions of the world as their anticipated "savior"?

With eighty nations represented in my parish, I am blessed with parishioners who are literally in touch with the world through their homelands. One such friend from India, Melchizedek Poniah, who teaches world religions in a nearby community college, handed me the March, 1992, issue of a small newspaper called *Hinduism Today*. Its masthead reads: "The Hindu Family Newspaper Affirming the Dharma and Recording the Modern History of Nearly a Billion Members of a Global Religion."

But it was the front-page headline that caught my eye: "India Awaits Vishnu's Return." The Hindus believe that we are living in the last age and that Vishnu, a member of the Hindu trinity, will return to this earth. Accordingly, there is "an increasingly large number of people who have begun to believe that the time has come for another birth in India of Lord Krishna. Lord Krishna said in the scripture *Bhagavad Gita* that whenever dharma [the way of righteousness] declined and it became beyond the capacity of human beings to put it back on the high pedestal it ought to occupy, He would re-incarnate Himself for accomplishing this task."

Again, does it sound familiar? When the woeful plight of humankind becomes so hopeless that there is no apparent way out, then will come the appearance of a "savior" to mend the ways of this lost planet. Catholics and Protestants long for Jesus. The Jews await the Messiah. Hindus look for Vishnu, their Lord Krishna. The Moslems believe that Allah will return someday soon. The Jains and Zoroastrians are expecting their gods.

It does not take a doctorate to conclude that Lucifer has masterfully set the stage across the planet for his final and overmastering delusion. What more effective strategy could there be than for him to come "transformed into an angel of light" and appear above the heartsick masses of humanity as the long-awaited Savior?

The Test

Do you have any concept of what it will be like to stand up against such a large global majority and quietly declare: "I do not believe that he is the Savior?" Imagine this being summoning you: "Come here, my son, my daughter—come, come, come to me. You don't believe me? O, Thomas of little faith, come here—touch my wounds and feel my scars. And blessed are those who, seeing, at last believe. But as for those who refuse to believe me, it would have been better that they had not been born; it would be better to tie a millstone around their necks and drown them in the depths of the sea." You see, Lucifer will selectively—as he did in the wilderness— quote the Scriptures and even Jesus Himself, all for his nefarious purpose of deceiving at last the whole world and Christendom to boot!

And then the desperate test and choice will confront us all: **Shall I believe my senses—or God's Scriptures?**

> Only those who have been diligent students of the Scriptures and who have received the love of the truth will be shielded from the powerful delusion that takes the world captive. By the Bible testimony these will detect the deceiver in his disguise. To all the testing time will come. By the sifting of temptation the genuine Christian will be revealed. Are the people of God so firmly established upon His Word that they would not yield to the evidence of their senses? Would they, in such a crisis, cling to the Bible and the Bible only? (*The Great Controversy*, p. 625.)

I think of how sensual—how sense-starved we have become. If the music doesn't have enough sensual appeal, we are dismayed. If worship isn't dramatic and entertaining and captivating enough, we feel let down. For we are the generation born and bred on the high-tech video pablum of Hollywood and Madison Avenue. We have become so saturated by the sensual that we, like lambs led to the slaughter, are duped by our senses more than we care to confess. Assaulted day and night by billboards, magazines, television, videos, stereos—the list is interminable.

What will happen to such a generation when the overpowering delusion in the end is the ultimate sensory experience—a mesmerizing monopoly of sight, sound, hearing, smell, and touch that makes even the thought of denying such evidence seem insane? How will we stand then, if we are not standing now?

It is just like the academic world. Every good student knows that you cannot fail all the quizzes and the midterm and still hope to pass the final in the end. It simply will not work! Now, I happen to know some students who have tried. Skipped the quizzes, forgot the homework, missed the labs, failed to study for the mid-term, and then tried to pass the final! Pass? Are you kidding! Because how you do on the big test at the end will be determined by how you did on the little tests along the way, right? I've been a student, and I've been a teacher. And we all know the law of academics: **To prepare for the big test, you must pass the small ones first.**

But you see, that's just it—there is someone else out there who doesn't want you to pass the small ones first. Because if he can keep you from preparing now, he can dupe you into failing then—in the end. Which is why *The Great Controversy* is so emphatic:

> The last great delusion is soon to open before us. So closely will the counterfeit resemble the true that it will be impossible to distinguish between them except by the Holy Scriptures. None but those who have fortified the mind with the truths of the Bible will stand through the last great conflict (p. 593).

None. N-o-n-e. Which makes that a terribly unpopular word and sentence, doesn't it? *"None but those who have fortified the mind with the truths of the Bible will stand through the last great conflict."*

I know what you're thinking: "I mean—come on, pastor. What are you trying to do? Discourage everybody from even trying at all?" No, not at all. But I'm wondering out loud how seriously some of us are taking the impending crisis. You see, years ago the church preached the Apocalypse and other sobering prophecies. But over the years a reaction began to develop against what came to be perceived as a negative focus: "After all, we're saved by faith, so that's all we need; and besides, it looks like a long time before these prophecies will ever come true anyway."

Well, I believe that the "long time" has at last passed. Of course, it is true that we are saved by faith in Jesus. The Apocalypse rings with that glorious truth! But there are too many today who are simply using the "gospel" as a front for a Casper Milquetoast kind of Christianity that—in standing for nothing—is falling for everything. You can whistle "Only Believe" until you're blue in the face; but if the faith of Jesus is not integrated into a passionate dependence upon Christ and a radical discipleship for Him, what good are all the catchy tunes and happy melodies in the world? Nobody dies for a whistle. The heroes and heroines of the Apocalypse have been and will continue to be those willing to die for what has so saturated their lives that, were they threatened with its loss, they would rather die. Hence the record: "They did not cling to life even in the face of death" (Revelation 12:11).

Dietrich Bonhoeffer, the young Lutheran pastor and theologian who was executed by Hitler at the end of World War II, wrote a soul-stirring sentence in his classic, *The Cost of Discipleship*: "When Christ calls a man, he bids him come and die." And so men and women have throughout the centuries. By the millions, Christian martyrs with a passionate faith in Jesus refused to bow before the icons of Caesar or the images of Rome. Will there be such a generation in this countdown to the showdown?

The Apocalypse is calling for one. It is not an accident that in the middle of chapters 12, 13, and 14, a clarion summons is sounded to an intensification of faith.

- **Chapter twelve:** "But they have conquered [the dragon] by the blood of the Lamb and by the word of their testimony, for they did not cling to life even in the face of death" (v. 11).

- **Chapter thirteen:** "Here is a call for the endurance and faith of the saints" (v. 10).

- **Chapter fourteen:** "Here is a call for the endurance of the saints, those who keep the commandments of God and hold fast to the faith of Jesus" (v. 12).

The Apocalypse is clear that it is only such an enduring faith that will shape the hearts and carry the lives of God's last generation through the final and nearly overmastering delusion.

Apparently the only way we will ever endure is by holding fast to Jesus. And just as apparently, you do not wait until the end to start holding on! There is an intensity in "holding fast" that this end-time church is going to have to get serious about if we are going to hold on until He comes.

I believe that a growing number of men and women and young adults and children across the nation and around the world are getting serious about holding fast. And my own heart bows before the evidence of what the Spirit of Christ is beginning to do among us, as He draws searching minds and hearts into a deeper study and knowledge of God through His Scriptures.

But what about those who seem oblivious to the impending crisis—whose lives seem to be caught up in the web of a value system that will one day disintegrate in the dust of the earth? What about those inside and outside our parishes, who—outwardly, at least—seem consumed with living for this moment and this moment alone? No preparation goes on in their lives for the future. No careful, prayerful, deeply personal kind of preparation takes place beyond the rote forms of religion. These seem not to know that the God of the Apocalypse is pleading with this civilization through a last message of mercy. And what—I ask with a concern fast becoming alarm—of these?

A Call to Prayer

Could it be that the time has come for us to pray for each other? Could it be that now is the right time for you to set aside a day of special prayer and fasting, as you earnestly seek the Spirit of God—for yourself, for your family and friends, for your community, for this dying civilization? And what would happen if you invited some others to join you— maybe even from the congregation where you worship? What if all of you decided together to set aside the same day, when through an intensity of prayer focus you would join together in supplicating the heart of our eternal Father for His promised blessing? Would God respond? Let Jesus Himself answer: "If you then, who are evil, know how to give good gifts to your children, how much more will the heavenly Father give the Holy Spirit to those who ask him!" (Luke 11:13).

"How *much more!*" It is that "much more" that our church and our world languish for today. "Ask and you will receive," Jesus promised in that same passage. Then shall we not ask? Or will James' declaration go on being true about us? "You do not have, because you do not ask" (James 4:2).

A few weeks ago our Pioneer Memorial Church parish joined together in a campus and community day of special prayer and fasting. We brought the following five-point prayer plan to God throughout that day and night of prayer. Isn't it a prayer list we could all join in praying in this critical hour of history?

> 1. That the Holy Spirit might be poured out in a deeper measure upon all of our hearts.

> 2. That those of us who do not yet sense the impending crisis might be gently led to see the utter and urgent need for preparing our souls—even *now*—for that day.

3. That all of us might be led during this year ahead into a deeper devotional and prayer experience with Christ.

4. That our timidities might be banished, and that, empowered by the Spirit, we might begin to tactfully but boldly share the good news of Jesus' soon return with others on the job, in the classroom, or about the neighborhood.

5. That God would show us how, earnestly and effectively, to build on the momentum of the Spirit across our community and around our world.

God Is Our Refuge

Now is the hour. God is ready to wrap up this last chapter of earth's history. But good news! It is not an hour for fear; it is a time for faith. Faith in the God of whom the psalmist declared in Psalm 46: "God is our refuge and strength, a very present help in trouble. Therefore we will not fear. . . . The Lord of hosts is with us, the God of Jacob is our refuge."

And that is why I am not afraid—nor should you be! Impending crisis? Yes. Overmastering delusion? Yes. All in the face of death? Yes. But we do not have to fear. For our God is with us. "God is our refuge and strength, a very present help in time of trouble."

Consider finally the story Llewellyn Wilcox told in his book, *Now Is the Time*. It is the story of a father and his little girl who fled into their private air-raid shelter in England during the height of the war. With the blitzkrieg overhead, it was apparent that the two of them must spend the night in that underground cubicle. Above them were death and destruction. Panic reigned, and the little girl was scared.

Father tucked her into one of the small cots in that shelter, then turned out the light and lay down on the cot against the other wall. But the girl couldn't sleep. The rumble overhead, the strangeness of an underground room she had never been in before, and the black shadows filled her with dreadful fears. Her mommy was gone. And she knew that above her in the night, many were dying. There in the darkness, she felt desperately lonely.

She didn't cry, but before long she couldn't stand it any longer, and she whispered across the room, "Daddy, are you there?"

"Yes, dear, I'm here; now go to sleep," was his quiet response.

She tried to, but she just couldn't. And before long that tiny voice spoke again, "Daddy, are you *still* there?"

Quick was his answer, "Yes, darling, I'm here. Don't be afraid, just go to sleep. It's all right." And for some time there was only silence, each lost in his or her own thoughts.

But finally, when the stillness and darkness were no longer bearable, the voice of the little one, craving reassurance, spoke the third time. "Daddy," she called out, "please tell me just one thing more: *Is your face turned this way?"*

And through the dark quickly there came the voice of her father in reply, "Yes, darling. Daddy is right here, and his face is turned your way." In an instant the girl fell asleep, in the perfect trust of a little child.

"God is our refuge and strength, a very present help in trouble. Therefore, we will not fear."

Good news for the impending crisis: **The face of our Father is turned our way.**

His face, we shall see much sooner than we think . . .

REVELATION 19 and 22

Then I saw heaven opened, and there was a white horse! Its rider is called Faithful and True, and in righteousness he judges and makes war.

His eyes are like a flame of fire, and on his head are many diadems; and he has a name inscribed that no one knows but himself.

He is clothed in a robe dipped in blood, and his name is called The Word of God.

And the armies of heaven, wearing fine linen, white and pure, were following him on white horses.

On his robe and on his thigh he has a name inscribed, "King of kings and Lord of lords."

"See, I am coming soon; my reward is with me, to repay according to everyone's work. I am the Alpha and the Omega, the first and the last, the beginning and the end."

The one who testifies to these things, says, "Surely I am coming soon."

Amen. Come, Lord Jesus! The grace of the Lord Jesus be with all the saints. Amen.

—Selected verses

7

I Saw Jesus Coming

I had a splitting headache—one of those Anacin 3 specials—as I twisted in my tangled sleeping bag, now tattered and muddied after nights on the soggy forest floor. Sleep? If you can call my restless tossing and rolling on the sloped earth and on that persecuting tree root that I couldn't escape *sleep*—then yes, I slept. But which of us out here in the benighted woods had really slept in days—or nights? I propped myself up on an elbow and peered into the gathering gloom. They were all there—humps wrapped tightly in their bags and curled against the mountain chill—my wife and two children and a few close friends. Fugitives, all of us. Homeless—and now hunted.

Trying to escape the pounding in my head, I groped in the black shadows for my radio. Jamming an earplug in, I twisted the tuner on my shortwave band. Soon the crackling voice of a crisp English accent repeated the BBC's world service headlines. With the chaos of our own national media and the recent government takeover of the major networks, the BBC proved to be our most reliable electronic window on the world.

A world, as the announcer intoned, fast collapsing—a world plunging cataclysmically into what now appeared to be utter planetary dysfunction and certain oblivion. The devastating global scourges that had racked the northern and southern hemispheres over recent months were now reported almost matter-of-factly. An oceanic plague more terrible than red tide had devastated the economies of coastal nations. On its heels had come the crimson contamination of fresh-water supplies on the land masses, and with the resultant drought, the agri-economic resources of the world's masses had shriveled away, producing global famine and starvation. A regular BBC feature now was its reporting on the bloody food riots in the world's great mega-cities. Rampant looting and mob carnage were twisting the last vestiges of civil order into a scarlet nightmare.

As a further result of this economic and ecological collapse, the socio-political fabric of human society was shredding faster than the newscasts could report it. The once-embraced values of human decency and dignity had long ago been cast to the raging winds of anarchy. The daily scene in most cities could only be described as a feeding frenzy. And adding to the gasping litany of doleful headlines was the deathly outbreak of a ravaging epidemic—a mysterious disease before which the medical community stood helpless. The onslaught of fear was no longer just endemic; it was now a global paralysis. The strained edge to the newscaster's voice mirrored the quiet terror that now gripped us with every snatch of news we were able to pick up here in our mountain hideaway.

It was all happening so fast! I glanced through the shadows to where my wife was still tossing. We had hoped we could weather the strident community reaction to our Sabbatarian convictions back home. We all knew that the president and the Congress, upheld by an expedited decision of the Supreme Court, were soon to ratify their national religious reform act. The New Christian Right had become the most powerful political coalition in our nation—the ultimate special-interest group. Their shotgun marriage with the Church of Rome led quickly and effectively to a lobbying blitz that secured the virtual abolition of our Bill of Rights—all, of course, in the national interests of God and moral revival.

I suppose that with the economic collapse and the social morass of our nation, it shouldn't have come as a surprise—the president's prime-time announcement. Thanks to CNN, his somber visage appeared on television screens worldwide. (I remembered how Ted Turner had said the day he launched CNN that barring technical problems, the network would broadcast "till the world ends." How prophetic his words now seemed!)

The president's sonorous voice had summoned Americans across "this great land to arise with one voice," as he put it, "to declare to the nations of this world that America has repented before God—that this land of the free shall rise up and lead the world in a renewed allegiance to the sovereign rule of Almighty God—an allegiance like that once possessed by our forefathers."

The national reaction had bordered on mass hysteria. A strange revival spread across the land with hypnotic speed. The few who raised lonely voices challenging the constitutionality of such a church and state amalgamation were quickly threatened and mysteriously silenced. When we awakened one morning soon after and discovered a scarlet cross and a threatening expletive splashed across our garage door, we knew that the time had come for our—as we told the neighbor—"short vacation out of town."

Four hundred miles northward and what seemed like months later, here we were. Sequestered along the edge of a jagged forest clearing on a mountainside we'd often come camping to in happier days long ago. How had the ancient prophet put it? "They will live on the heights; their refuge will be the fortresses of the rocks; their food will be supplied, their water assured" (Isaiah 33:16). And indeed God had not forsaken us. For strangely enough, the stream beside which we now lay huddled hadn't turned into the contaminated crimson the radio reported. And in the undergrowth beneath the towering forest, we had scrounged enough food to stave off starvation. Food and water for our fugitive stomachs.

But it was our hearts that were knotted now, twisted by the dark foreboding that perhaps even yet, after all the exploding fulfillments of the Apocalypse in the sobering headlines over our crackling radio—that even after all of this, our clinging faith in God might fail and our trembling hope in Jesus might crumble. What if we should let Him down in the very end? The worrisome question was another reason no one slept much on the soggy ground. Through the night watches, we would often huddle close to each other, the knees of our dirty jeans worn brown from pleading with the God who reigned beyond the stars. If only He might—as He did in that dark midnight with Jacob—speak a quiet word of grace, of forgiveness, of mercy, of a salvation and hope beyond our seemingly impending deaths.

For already, both the shortwave and regional stations we picked up were trumpeting the new international decree. Shaped by the confederation of governments and religions whose nuncios and ambassadors were meeting in Rome, it declared the unilateral and summary eradication of the "spiritual hemorrhaging that threatens humankind." Meaning conscientious objectors such as we were. Death for those who stubbornly and senselessly persisted in defying the world's collective will had been decreed for midnight.

What happened next transpired with blinding speed. I had just jerked the earplug out when I heard a distant rumble below us. The sound of all-terrain engines, whining up the forest floor. And then voices. Sharp commands. Our hiding place had been found!

In that instant of terror as we scrambled and clawed up

the mountainous slope in the darkness of midnight, it was suddenly as if time stood still. "The seventh angel poured his bowl into the air, and a loud voice came out of the temple, from the throne, saying, 'It is done!' And there came flashes of lightning, rumblings, peals of thunder, and a violent earthquake, such as had not occurred since people were upon the earth, so violent was that earthquake" (Revelation 16:17, 18).

Like a splattered watermelon, the earth beneath our feet broke open. And in a single instant the entire planet fissured, the globe collapsing like the Oakland freeway in the San Francisco earthquake. "The sky vanished like a scroll rolling itself up, and every mountain and island was removed from its place" (Revelation 6:14).

Now it is as if nature has gone berserk. Suddenly the blinding sun mysteriously appears—and *at midnight!* Mountain rocks hurl down their slopes, crashing into forests and exploding onto plains below, decimating everything in their pathway. The still-scarlet ocean boils into mountainous walls of tsunamis—killer waves that lash entire island chains of life into oblivion. The very air of the ruptured heavens is set afire by sheets of white and yellow lightning that strike the dusty earth bed into a million fires burning in a night turned frantic day.

And in that solitary moment, earth's proud bastions of defiance—the seaport cities of the world—are reduced to flotsam, swept away by an avenging sea. The temples of glass and steel and mortar and stone, once boastful icons of human ingenuity and rebellion—the skyscrapers of the world's sprawling cities—collapse like a house of cards before the rolling, heaving earth, an earth that has suffered long under the iron fist of human exploitation. Now as if to rid itself of its destroying virus, it heaves and wretches like an addict beside a night street lamp. And into the night they wail, the distant sirens of disaster—tornado and hurricane and nuclear warning sirens tripped by the pitching of the earth. Their eerie moans rise into the thickened sky above to join the raging cacophony of destruction, "like the voice of demons upon a mission of destruction" (*The Great Contro-versy*, p. 637).

We scramble to a higher outcropping on the mountain slope. No one knows for certain any longer whether it is night or day. The sky above is choked with dark, belching smoke that rises like an atomic mushroom cloud from the valley floor below us. All the red and black and orange images of Kuwait's oilfield infernos cannot compare to the thick, smelly carnage of destruction that now billows up from the crumpled earth below. Tiny dots of red and blue flash wildly through the smoke from the distant cities—emergency vehicles that can never stanch earth's last hemorrhaging.

And then someone shouts. And our hearts stop. For from our rocky ledge, we can see it—the sign that countless generations of this race have passed on to their children—the sure and certain sign that humanity's wildest hopes are about to come true: "In the east a small black cloud, about half the size of a man's hand" (*Ibid.*, p. 640).

With solemn awe, our eyes are riveted to that growing cloud. Black, yet gold around its mushrooming edges, it moves in from the east and seems to throb with every expanding billow. Closer and closer—brighter and brighter. The black has been but a shadow, for now as it expands to fill the heavens, the cloud has turned white—a brilliant fire white that shines like the noon-day sun. To the east and west and north and south, the flaming cloud flows and spills into every niche of heaven.

And then above the screaming earth we hear it—the sound of music. The cloud is alive! "With mighty chariotry, twice ten thousand, thousands upon thousands, the Lord came!" (Psalm 68:17). Beings of light. Tall and noble. Singing a majestic rhapsody that tingles up our backs. Though we can't make out their words, high atop that ledge there stirs within our souls an echoing refrain.

But our own paean is not set free until that moment when our eyes are drawn still upward, higher still. And there in that cumulus of fire, *He rides!* "His eyes are like a flame of

fire, and on his head are many diadems. He is clothed in a
robe dipped in blood, and the armies of heaven, wearing fine
linen, white and pure, were following him on white horses.
On his robe he has a name inscribed, 'King of kings and Lord
of lords'" (Revelation 19:12, 13, 16).

Someone half yells, half whispers, "It's Jesus!" And like
an unchained melody, our ecstatic cries ascend to heaven.
"This same Jesus" has come at last for us! Weeping with joy
and laughing through our tears, we instinctively clasp each
other in glad embrace. "Lo, this is our God; we have waited
for him, so that he might save us. Let us be glad and rejoice
in his salvation" (Isaiah 25:9).

Closer and closer He comes. And then in a moment that
will never be forgotten, the Prince of Heaven stretches out
His purple-scarred hands and with a shout that thunders like
music through the corridors of the sky, Jesus cries, "Awake,
you who sleep in the dust—and arise!" And on a thousand
forgotten hills and from a myriad of abandoned cemeteries,
the best comes last! High in the reeling sky is heard the
clarion silver blast of a trumpet. And in a single spinning
moment, the dusty covers of a billion beds are thrown back,
and the sleeping friends of God awaken. No sooner has that
piercing bugle sounded, than there is movement to our side.
Instinctively, we turn to fully face one of heaven's proud
warriors. Cradled in his strong arms we see the cooing,
delighted smile of the precious little daughter we buried in
unknowable heartbreak on a day long ago on a faraway
hillside. And in a blur of tears, our lives are healed at last.

"Beam me up, Scotty!" was how the world had once
dreamed it. But in this magic moment, it all comes true.
Suddenly they materialize all around us—those angelic
guardians who all our lives have lived unseen beside us.
With flashing eyes that beckon in smiling welcome, they take
our hands and—with the thrill of a Sears Tower elevator
ride—beam us upward, higher and higher into the now-
chilled sky. And not just our little cluster. With awe we crane
our necks to scan the purple and white of the orange sky—

and we see them. We are surrounded by millions of others—men and women and boys and girls and babies and teenagers and families and friends and strangers with the kindest faces—soaring, all of us together, up from gaping graveyards and shattered horizons, up from sea and land, up from hovel and dungeon. A billion beaming faces from every "nation and kindred and tongue and people," every shining eye still locked onto the beckoning face of Jesus, His flowing white hair and youthful countenance turned toward us, His arms and nail-scarred hands outstretched in an embracing welcome, His flaming dark eyes smiling silently, "I told you I'd come back for you!"

Higher and higher into the deep purple of space and toward the exploding cloud of light we ascend. The blue-green ball below, so long our terrestrial home, recedes beneath our soaring feet. They say that home is where the heart is. Gazing now into the approaching face of Jesus, everything within us cries out, "We are home at last!"

"Even so, come, Lord Jesus. Amen."

Afterword

So where do we go from here? "From here to eternity," someone once wrote. And of course, that isn't such a bad idea—eternity, I mean. For surely the heart of every reader of the Apocalypse will ever be confronted with the fiery hope of a soon-coming Savior. Eternity, indeed! And the sooner, the better.

But lest somehow we might surmise that the only alternative left for us in a morally bankrupt and rapidly sinking society is to abandon the world and flee to the hills to await our Lord there, may I remind you that the primitive church also hoped for the soon coming of Jesus? And how did they live out their hopes? Was it not in the unfettered witness they proclaimed in the midst of their own decadent society?

Peter and Mary and Paul and Joanna and Luke and Thomas and Mark and Rhoda—the Book of Acts shines with the iridescent glow of their personal testimony about Jesus and their public witness to His truth. Along the boulevards and alleyways of their great urban centers, in the political forum as well as the private rendezvous, there they could be found, the everlasting gospel of the Apocalypse upon their lips.

Must it not be the same for the church at the end? Hasn't the time come for us to follow in their crimson steps—to live out the witness of the primitive church in these apocalyptic times? Is this not also our mission—we who are so easily intimidated by our own foolish pride: "What will the neighbors think of me?" Isn't it time we asked instead, "What do they think of Jesus?" Hasn't the time come for us to forsake our affluent and sophisticated reserve and with abandon cast our lives in the furrow of this world's desperate need to know the truth about God?

What difference does it make what they think of us? The fire-cast glow along the crumbling horizon of time is proof enough that if we don't share what we've discovered in Jesus now, we may never have the chance again! God isn't calling us to the hills—He's compelling us into the highways and byways of the human race in this waning hour—a race to the finish.

In the face of the dwindling commodity of time, we need the rekindling commitment of the Spirit. "But you will receive power when the Holy Spirit has come upon you; and you will be my witnesses . . . to the ends of the earth" (Acts 1:8). And that's a promise. "You *will* receive." No ifs, ands, or buts about Jesus' parting gift 2,000 years ago—the very gift of Spirit-power we so desperately need on the eve of Christ's return. So let us ask—and ask and ask and ask again.

For to you and me—the readers of the Apocalypse and disciples of the Master—has come the urgent summons: Go! Into a dying world with a living hope. Go! The passionate commission of our apocalyptic Lord. Go! Even if no one else goes. Go! The time has come for us to go.

"And remember, I am with you always, to the end of the age" (Matthew 28:20).